I AM
RESPONSIBLE:
The Hand of AA

Selected Stories from the AA Grapevine

The AA Grapevine, Inc.
New York, New York
www.aagrapevine.org

Responsibility Declaration

I am responsible. When anyone, anywhere
reaches out for help, I want the hand of AA
always to be there. And for that:

I am responsible.

AA Preamble

Alcoholics Anonymous
is a fellowship of men and women who share
their experience, strength and hope with each other
that they may solve their common problem and
help others to recover from alcoholism.
The only requirement for membership is a desire
to stop drinking. There are no dues or fees for
AA membership; we are self-supporting through our
own contributions. AA is not allied with any sect,
denomination, politics, organization or institution;
does not wish to engage in any controversy; neither
endorses nor opposes any causes. Our primary purpose
is to stay sober and help other alcoholics
to achieve sobriety.

Contents

Contents continued

Foreword

When AA's Responsibility Declaration was presented to the Fellowship at the 30th International Convention in Toronto, Canada, in 1965, it gave voice to the deep and abiding aspiration of recovering alcoholics around the world. In just a few simple words, it captured the essence of the Fellowship — one alcoholic sharing with another — and provided a fundamental building block for the future of the Fellowship. One hand reaching out for the next — a chain reaction of help, healing, and hope.

For those who have reached out for help, alone and afraid, and been met with the firm, supportive hand of AA, the Responsibility Declaration is an emblem of the lifeline that saved them. And for those AAs, sober now, who have taken that outstretched hand into their own, the Declaration is but one small installment on the debt each owes to the Fellowship of AA.

The thirty-eight stories in this volume take a look at the impact of AA's Responsibility Declaration and what it means to individuals and to the Fellowship as a whole. Written by AA members and nonalcoholic friends of the Fellowship, the articles explore what it's like to take responsibility, for ourselves and for others. Carrying the message to those who still suffer, learning how to stay sober ourselves, and finding ways to keep AA alive and growing are the principal activities that consume us as AA members. As we extend the hand of AA, responsibility becomes the bedrock upon which happy and purposeful lives can be built.

To set the stage for the stories in this volume, we present some opening thoughts from AA's co-founder, Bill W., writing from the vantage point of AA's twenty-fifth anniversary, sharing his perspective on AA's progress and prospects for the future. In this visionary article, "The Shape of Things to Come," Bill says: "While we need not alter our basic truths, we can surely improve their application to ourselves, to AA as a whole, and to our relation with the world around us. We can constantly step up 'the practice of these principles in all our affairs.'"

And for that, we are all responsible.

~⤳~

Introduction

The Shape of Things to Come

AA's first quarter-century is now history. Our next twenty-five years lie in prospect before us. How, then, can we make the most of this new grant of time?

Perhaps our very first realization should be that we can't stand still. Now that our basic principles seem established, now that our functioning is fairly effective and widespread, it would be temptingly easy to settle down as merely one more useful agency on the world scene. We could conclude that "AA is fine, just the way it is."

Yet how many of us, for example, would presume to declare, "Well, I'm sober and I'm happy. What more can I want, or do? I'm fine the way I am." We know that the price of such self-satisfaction is an inevitable backslide, punctuated at some point by a very rude awakening. We have to grow or else deteriorate. For us, the "status quo" can only be for today, never for tomorrow. Change we must; we cannot stand still.

Just how, then, can AA go on changing for the better? Does this mean that we are to tinker with our basic principles? Should we try to amend our Twelve Steps and Twelve Traditions? Here the answer would seem to be "no." Those twenty-four principles have first liberated us, have then held us in unity, and have enabled us to function and to grow as AA members, and as a whole. Of course perfect truth is surely something better understood by God than by any of us. Nevertheless we have come to believe that AA's recovery Steps and Traditions do represent the approximate truths which we need for our particular purpose. The more we practice them, the more we like them. So there is little doubt that AA principles continue to be advocated in the form they stand now.

So then, if our basics are so firmly fixed as all this, what is there left to change or to improve? The answer will immediately occur to us. While we need not alter our truths, *we can surely improve their application to ourselves, to AA as a whole, and to our relation with the world around us.* We can constantly step up "the practice of these principles in all our affairs."

As we now enter upon the next great phase of AA's life, let us therefore re-dedicate ourselves to an ever greater responsibility for our general welfare. Let us continue to take our inventory as a fellowship, searching out our flaws and confessing them freely. Let us devote ourselves to the repair of all faulty relations that may exist, whether within or without.

And above all, let us remember that great legion who still suffer from alcoholism and who are still without hope. Let us, at any cost or sacrifice, so improve our communication with all these that they may find what we have found — a new life of freedom under God.

Bill W.
AA Grapevine
February 1961

~~

Section One

Carrying the Message

You have to give it away to keep it" is a phrase often heard around
the rooms of AA, or, as Bill W. put it in the July 1955 Grapevine,
"We must carry the message, else we ourselves can wither and those
who haven't been given the truth will die."

Clearly, AA is a lifesaving proposition. We have to carry the
message to other alcoholics — for their benefit and ours. It matters
little who they are or where they come from. What matters is that we
extend the hand of AA, the only lifeline some alcoholics will ever
know.

It's not always pretty, and going on a Twelfth Step call or working
with a wet drunk may not be easy or fun. Yet in the great paradox of
AA, it is in freely giving that we find our own reward.

Here is how that reward is pictured in *Twelve Steps and Twelve
Traditions,* a collection of articles on what it means to practice the
principles of AA:

"To watch the eyes of men and women open with wonder as they
move from darkness into light, to see their lives quickly fill with new
purpose and meaning, to see whole families reassembled, to see the
alcoholic outcast received back into his community in full citizenship,
and above all to watch these people awaken to the presence of a loving
God in their lives — these things are the substance of what we receive
as we carry AA's message to the next alcoholic."

A Dose of Reality

I recently went on a Twelfth Step call with another recovering alcoholic to a woman's home. What I saw and felt there is almost impossible to put into words, but I felt the need to try for those in the Fellowship who may be getting somewhat complacent. After many years of sobriety it's easy to remember, but not always feel, the depth of the pain. This experience flooded my soul with the reality of the disease.

As my friend and I entered the apartment, we were met with the stench of vomit and urine. The woman was covered with filth. She was partially nude, she was malnourished, there was no food in the house, bills were gathering dust. Two bottles of whiskey were at her bedside. With this chaos around her, all this poor woman could ask for, beg for, was another drink.

Amidst this disarray and sickness, on her stark walls was evidence of her past life: hanging in a beautiful frame was a "Mother of the Year" award.

This woman altered my life. Although I didn't reach the depths of despair that she did, it is waiting for me if I drink again.

I thank God for a daily reprieve contingent on my spirituality. Because of this woman, I pray longer, help others more, read AA literature with a vengeance, and try to apply the Steps more avidly. I don't know if I helped her, but she will never know how much she helped me.

Jill L.
York, Pennsylvania
September 1999

Nobody's Sweetheart

A lcoholism corrupted all of my emotions. It denied me love, compassion, and concern for those around me. In place of these spiritual impulses were lust, sentimentality, and distrust. Only after I found recovery did I begin to know the meaning of love.

My first real experience of love was the caring given me when I was introduced to AA. I was too close to my last drink to appreciate the concern, but knew I had to stick around. There wasn't any place left to go.

A couple of days after my first meeting, I was in an Alano Club spilling coffee and trying to figure out how I was going to put my life back together. One of the old-timers brought in an antagonistic wet drunk. This guy was nobody's sweetheart. He was a know-it-all loud-mouth who could not be pleased. He was critical of everyone and everything. While he ranted and railed against all he saw, his new sponsor made phone calls to various sober halfway houses to find a bed for him. One was located, and a collection was taken up for his first week's rent. He was ushered into a car and driven off.

That afternoon I had seen the only kind of love there is, uncondi-tional love. The love shown by the old-timers did not depend on the drunk's ability to accept it. They simply expressed, through action, the love they had been given. They had no need to hear any gratitude from the drunk — drunks aren't often grateful. They didn't expect to hear an honest appraisal of his situation—an honest drunk is hard to find. They certainly did not expect a sincere promise to abstain for-ever—the "sincerity" requirement for membership had been dropped long ago. They merely did the things necessary to start him on his road of happy destiny.

I was overwhelmed and shaken by what I saw — visibly so. Another old-timer saw my situation and took me to a little side room

9

where we talked. I began to sob from a great sense of relief. I could see that the love shown to the wet drunk had been shown to me, and I hadn't recognized it until now. I also knew I would never have to drink again.

Our conversation was simple. My new friend asked when I had had my last drink, when I had eaten last, and if I was sleeping indoors that night. He told me his story; he had drunk up his soul, found Alcoholics Anonymous, and had not had a drink since. My hope was strengthened even more, and I knew I had found a way to live without booze.

The story of that afternoon, and many like it, convince me that God's love is expressed through action. It has been the actions of others that has given me unfailing support throughout my sobriety. It also shows how I am to respond to those whom I can help. I am responsible to see that the hand of AA is available to anyone.

I'm not sure what happened to the wet drunk. He graduated from the sober house and found a job. I saw him at meetings regularly until I left the area. I hope he's still sober. I know I am, and a part of that is owed to him.

Anonymous
Moreno Valley, California
December 1992

∽

Accepting the Invitation

I was sitting in my usual spot when the call came in. My mind was drifting into those recesses where fear, anger, and frustration lurk.

When my sponsee asked me to go on a Twelfth Step call with her, I said "sure" at once, because that is what I had been taught and I wanted to make sure she got the same lesson: "When anyone, anywhere reaches out for help, I want the hand of AA always to be there. And for that: I am responsible."

We were told the lady was in a local motel and that she had many years in the program. My mind jumped around to what could I possibly say to someone with that many years and me so few. What happened? Did she quit going to meetings? Did she not do inventories? Did she isolate? All those warnings I heard in meetings, came rolling over me.

My sponsee and I said our prayers and asked God to guide us and give us the words to help the poor, distressed lady.

When she opened the door to the motel room, all I saw was an older lady who was in obvious emotional, spiritual pain, and my first reaction was, as it has always been: to put my arms around her and give her a big hug.

She had recently lost a spouse and was coming through our state on her way back home after the burial. Her grief had reached a point at which she needed to talk to another AA woman to help her through her pain so that she could continue her journey.

My sponsee and I listened while she shared with us her experience, strength, and hope, and especially her pain. I was able to share with her the grief I felt (and still feel) for the loss of my father. Together our burdens were lifted.

As we sat sharing, one alcoholic to another, we saw that beautiful transformation in our lady as strength and courage straightened her back and the smile slowly crept into her face. Our lady had not had an alcohol relapse, but rather an emotional relapse. Fortunately, though, her time in the program gave her the sure knowledge of where to find help before she picked up a drink.

I knew I had been given a special gift. The lady is now a part of my life and it doesn't matter if our paths never cross again. In my God's giant jigsaw puzzle, our pieces were fitted together just for that brief moment in time and my life was changed.

My sponsor told me early in sobriety, "Accept the invitation and you will grow." I accepted the invitation to go on a Twelfth Step call and I in turn was twelfth-stepped.

Jolene N.
Okmulgee, Oklahoma
May 1994

∾

Oh God, You Again?

Never go on a Twelfth Step call alone," Emery tells me. We're at the old clubhouse on Twenty-third Street in New York. I have thirty days' sobriety. Emery's my sponsor.

"Not with an active drunk," he says. "It doesn't pay. Believe me, two guys leaning on a drunk is 150 percent more than one guy leaning on a drunk."

John S.'s married daughter has come into the clubhouse looking for Emery. Her dad has slipped and is holed up in the Hotel Albert in the Village. He's out of booze and threatens to kill himself if she doesn't return with a fifth to fight off his blue devils. Emery's been through this before with John, a career noncom now cashiered after nearly thirty years of duty stations with the Army paymaster's office.

"John gets the message, but then he just can't hold onto it. Too much slippery elm on his brain cells," Em says. Emery's a fair-headed Missouri boy and big as a quarterback. "Well, saddle up, pilgrim. We go forth to do the Lord's work."

Near the Albert, he guides me into a liquor store.

"We may need a medicinal pint, if words don't work. And if I know John." He eyes the shelves. We buy the cheapest and head into the Albert.

The Albert is one step up from a Bowery flop but somehow worse, a sinktrap for unbearable depression. Hard sadness sighs from a hundred rooms. The halls smell like clams. My neck creaks. I feel drowsy, sluggish, grief-stricken.

Em knocks on John's door.

"Hey, John! Wake up. The troops have landed."

"Door's open," John husks within.

Darkness puddles his room. Death-fall and shade down. The walls, bed, chair, and table are simply a dough gray glow.

"Oh God," John says from his pillow. "You again. Why have you come here?"

A tech/sergeant's jacket on the chair hangs weighted with countless years of travel, service, stripes, ribbons, hash-marks. The poisonous room echoes with the helpless cries of former tenants. It is a tank of viruses and stinks of innertube lungs and wretched bowel gas.

"D'ya mind if we breathe some fresh air, John?"

John groans.

Em lifts the shade and opens the window. John turns from the gray light as a great sucking of sighs goes up the airshaft. His pale red hair sticks to freckled, doughy flesh. Do I see two Johns, slightly disjointed, a live spirit struggling in a dead body — or a dead spirit in a quivering body?

"Get outta here," he whispers to the wall.

"This mist was once a living man," Em tells me. "Hey, John, aren't you tired of your damned loathsomeness?"

John's parched hand shakes at Em as if shriveled by electric current. "Shut up!"

"You don't have to lay in the same sheets all month, John. They'll change 'em for ya every week if ya let the maid in. So how ya feelin? We missed ya at the clubhouse."

"I can't tawgg. . ."

"Sounds like you been sucking on sandpaper. Frankly, I marvel at your composure, considering the shape you're in. I brought my friend Donald. He's a recovering drunk too."

John smiles, horridly. "How long you been sober?"

"Thirty days."

"See that?" Em cries. "It can be done. Thirty days ago he was as degenerate as you, John."

I gaze about Suicide's Seabottom.

"I get along," John says. But his dreadful voice is a cow's tongue up my back.

John wheezes, his lungs gluefilled saddlebags. His hand shakes or punches at us. "Coughin' myself t'death!"

"Next thing ya'll tell me, ya need a drink," Em says.

John chokes as his eyes race between us hopefully, his fist at his mouth. "I think I been coughin' for forty years. Either of you guys got a rainy-day heel o'the dog?"

"Donald, I droop! We'll never win this guy. And the horrible thing is, this human mess is my Higher Power. Can you believe he's the reason I'm in our spiritual organization?"

John begs me prayerfully. I'm ready to break out the bottle in my shopping bag. But Em stays my hand.

"I'm telling ya, you don't need a drink," Em says. "Are you seeing bugs? Or strange people walking around in here? There's a glorious truth I'm trying to work through your fog. Listen to me! You condemned yourself to this rathole. But you have the power in you to rise up outta this foulness and inta the light."

"You make me cry."

"I'm sure I do. Do you hear this genius, Donald? Thinks he'd got me over a barrel. Well, I'm here to help you, John. But first ya gotta show an earnest inclination."

"I don't know what you're talking about."

"Oh, get with it, meatball. John, the world has advanced whole decades since you left it. You haven't the slightest glimmer of the great advances sobriety has wrought upon this country. Diseases have been conquered. New York's had two World's Fairs. And you've missed it all."

"I'm no hick, don't insult me. Either of you guys got any money?

If not, vamoose."

"What year is this, Einstein?" Em asks.

"I know what year it is."

"Who's president now? That's another popular question."

"Ha! Who cares?"

"What city are you in?"

"I know where I am."

"If you knew where you were, you wouldn't be here."

"We're in Biloxi. There, there, ya fruitcake!"

My despair swells. The room dims alarmingly. A cloud over the airshaft? What the hell is a dewy-eyed young man like me doing here? Beside John I'm not even a drunk.

Em eyes the shopping bag long and silently.

"Now shut up and listen," Em says, "Don'tcha think it's time ya gave yourself a rest? I mean a real rest."

"I got a bed. Right here."

"But you're not sleeping, are you?"

"Who could sleep in this circus?"

"Circus? I'd say this place is about as noisy as the grave. And just about as consoling. You know, John, I know just the quiet place you need. Nice place in the country. Sort of a halfway house, more of a rehab. Guy who runs it dearly loves working with drunks. How'd ya like to see real land again? Sleep under a real roof in a real house out where it's quiet and all ya hear are birds and crickets and singin' frogs? Like t'try it? Speak up!"

John coughs himself purple.

"I might! He got any moonshine?"

"Who?"

"This farmer."

"He's just got well-water. Good God-given well water. You can have a bath too, scrape some of that scum off. You want a hot bath before ya slide inta those fresh-smelling cool sheets on that big double-bed, don'tcha?"

John dims with dread. Must he give up this room? Something comes over his face. Touch him and he bruises, his scalp is bruised and arms blotched with broken capillaries. He feels warped, armless, legless, useless? I would in his place.

John says, "What does he know about me?"

"All he knows about you is that you lost faith in yourself."

"Yeah? How does he know that? Does he think he's God?"

"John, you been drunk a long time. Now you gotta trust in nature to restore you. Can society rebuild you? Of course not."

"Society sucks," I suggest.

"But, John, other people can help us rebuild ourselves. Other people who have had our illness and lived through it. There's something about being part of a bunch of people all turned in the same direction, toward the sun, you might say, that restores us. The force that heals a burnt forest can as surely heal us. Do you want to hear this? I don't have any booze. I do have a big cheapo jar of antacid tablets that I find sorta soothing, and just as good as ice cream as a relaxant and sedative. Would you like some tablets?"

John watches Em unscrew a large jar from the shopping bag.

"These are placebos?" John says.

"What if they are, as long as they fit the hangover? And they do. Now, are you ready for the pitch?"

"I've heard it before."

"And you keep forgetting it! This is serious stuff, John. It could realign your genes for you. But I can only tell you how it works for me. When I drink in the closet, my dog gets very upset. Because he can smell me right through the door and he doesn't like me when I'm drinking. He thinks I'm all starry-eyed and cuckoo.

"Look here, John. Of the two of us, which one will walk out of this room and go home to a warm woman and find himself enjoying the good life his Higher Power means him to have?"

"Just because you're better off than I am right now doesn't mean diddly about a Higher Power. You could be in a state of bustitude with me tomorrow. Ha!"

"And the wondrous mystery is that I'm not there with you right now. John, I'll climb a hill and look at the stars while you dig your own grave. It's up to you. Your choice. For me, recovery is other people. Faith in a group's power to energize me, why should I knock that? I'm not whistling 'Dixie,' I'm talking full recovery. You aren't just a waterlogged tree trunk rolling in the surf. You have purpose. Your recovery. Believe me, two men together is a greater force than two men apart. And the same goes for the energy and spirit of a group. You want to join us again? We have a spiritual purpose: to help each other help ourselves. Men together act powerfully on each other and give off those big vibes."

"Big vibes, huh? I prefer to be alone."

"Of course you do. And you prefer sucking your thumb. You've had long practice at it. Why would we expect anything else from you? I like being alone! Only in solitude are we still enough for our inner being to speak to us. Fishing is nice like that, real spiritual. Fly fishing, I mean. We can't grow without giving ourselves space for silence and the voice within. But you want to know what you are, John? You're absolutely hopeless. And when a drunk is as hopeless as you, he becomes brittle. Ready to snap. The perfect target for recovery. He has no place else to go. If necessary, I will responsor you. But I warn you right now. I've had my failures. One-on-one Twelfth Step calls like this one that ended up in funerals. They weigh on me. I should lighten up on myself, especially with hopeless cases, the kind I really welcome. Some people just snap, and give recovery a half-assed shot, then drink some isopropyl or drop dead in the summer sun. We get such damn hot summers that these sitting ducks only get half of the message. They grumble and come to meetings just to prolong their self-infatuation. Even a Missouri boy can spot this. It's the other half of the message that's so hard for them. This is where you ask me, What half is that?"

"What half is that, hayseed?"

17

Em shrugs. "Giving it away. Ya gotta give it away to have it. Be part of the pipeline. Recovery is giving it away. If you don't give it away you can't have it. That's the secret. Getting your thumb out of your mouth and thinking about others, just as I'm thinking about you. Which, like I say, is a wondrous mystery. It's nice that you may be getting something out of this, and I hope you do. But I am sitting in this room talking to myself, not to you, John. I am a practical man, I'm from Missouri. You're only where I would be if I wasn't talking with you. This is a selfish program based on brotherly love. And I want to thank you and your illness for keeping me sober. I hope you don't think I'm being too gushy. I have a mean side that carries me away sometimes and I have to avoid sounding harsh."

"Yeah? Well, you frighten me, buster. Where is that farm you were talking about?"

"John, rise up and walk. We'll look through the farm files at intergroup. Donald, do you have something in that bag for John?"

"How about some more tablets, John?"

"Hell, give him the whole jar of antacid," Em says. "He can carry it around with him like a warm blanket."

John disengages from the mist he lies in and we help him up. Sick waves of the Albert cling to him like wriggling viruses. But a cloud clears the airshaft. John's face is salt tossed in sunlight.

"But we're heaving you inta the shower before we go anywhere, fella," Em says. Then he whispers to me, "Like trying t'save Genghis Khan, wasn't it?"

Don N.
Greenwich Village, New York
December 1997

⮾

The Hate-and-Pain Guy

The other day I was trying to remember what the actual turning point for me in the program was. I think it was when I really started to get into service work, and, specifically, taking meetings into institutions.

The first time I went into a prison was when this old-timer, Vic, invited me to go with a group of guys from my home group to a meeting at Sheridan Federal Prison. I was really surprised at how good an AA meeting it was. I mean, there was a clear topic, everyone seemed to take it pretty seriously, all the guys seemed to be well versed in the program, and I got a lot out of everyone's talks. I probably was the only weak link in the whole thing. With two years sober, I was one of the newest guys to AA at that meeting. Since most of the guys in Sheridan were doing pretty long stretches of time, and a lot of the guys started going to AA not too long after they got in, several of them had five to ten years of sobriety. And I thought I was going to be schooling the poor inmates on how to stay sober. Man, I had a lot to learn.

Every meeting I went to, I gained more respect for the guys in that group. They had their own secretary and chairperson. They were sponsoring each other and going through the Steps. I also found out that inmates going to an AA meeting in a federal prison weren't real popular. I guess it made the guys suspect you of being a narc. If you were trying to change your life for the better, and in the process you were refusing to drink any homemade pruno or to take any yard drugs, all the other inmates thought you might be the kind of guy who would rat them out. So a lot of the guys were walking the yard pretty much alone. Yet they still came. And they taught me so much. I tried to show them that a guy could stay sober out on the streets, and they showed me how to live an honorable life even in a place where you were considered just a number.

I started to go in pretty regularly with my buddy George, who was the Oregon area coordinator for Sheridan. That was until George started to get very ill and the meetings at the prison began to fall off. George ended up in the hospital with cancer and endstage diabetes a couple months later. I remember getting guilt-tripped by one of the guys in our group to go visit him in the hospital. Man, I hated hospitals — all those sick people. But I went, and there was George in the cancer ward with his foot half amputated, given only a month or so to live. Angel (a friend of ours who helped start the AA meetings out at Sheridan from the inside and who had since gotten out and become a big part of our local AA community) was also there visiting George. It was all a bit too gloomy for my taste. George proceeded to deliver a classic deathbed request. He asked me if I would take over for him as the coordinator for Sheridan. He went into a long, moving speech about how it had been his life's work for the past eight years, how I was the only one who really knew the clearance system, and how it would put his heart at ease to know that someone who really cared was taking it over for him. Of course, I fell for it, not being nearly as savvy as I had thought I was. They both started laughing hysterically. Even worse was bumping into the shift nurse as I was leaving and hearing her say that George got visitors all day long, that there was constant laughter coming from his room, and that he was the only patient they could remember on the cancer ward who laughed so much. Well, George finally passed away, laughing to the very end, and I ended up taking a couple of meetings a month into Sheridan.

It took me a while to get the hang of this new service commitment, but I really enjoyed the meetings out at the prison. Oh, and there was that other little benefit: I hadn't taken a drink in quite some time. I became pretty good friends with most of the regulars at the meeting, and I could spot a new guy a mile away. One in particular, Garvar, began to catch my attention. He was a real muscular guy with tattoos from head to toe (not that that really distinguished him in the joint).

He was very quiet and seemed to have a constant undercurrent of anger about him. But he seemed really serious about the program and was always very attentive at the meetings. Even though he wasn't all that social a guy at the beginning, we seemed to hit it off right from the start. As time went on, Garv (or the Hate-and-Pain Guy, as some volunteers at first called him because he had "hate" and "pain" tattooed across his knuckles) began to loosen up in the meetings and became a real part of the home group.

A couple of years went by, and Garv was about to get out of prison. To my surprise, he decided to relocate to the Eugene area, as Angel had some five years back. I guess that because he had gotten to know several of us volunteers from the Eugene area, he felt it would be better to hang with us rather than with his old running buddies back in L.A. I soon was bumping into him around town at the meetings the halfway house let him attend. A few months later, he was out altogether.

Garv eventually asked me to sponsor him, and I agreed with some reservations. I had sponsored guys before, but no one with his sort of background and years in the joint. So I was a bit concerned that we wouldn't be able to relate about those issues. I thought maybe he should look for someone who had done some time in prison to sponsor him. But we figured if it wasn't working out, he could find someone else down the road.

At the beginning, Garv was real uncomfortable on the outside. There were all these new personalities to deal with. And worse yet, there were all these damn details of life — driver's license, rent, taxes, all sorts of applications. I don't think either of us was sure he was going to make it. I think he thought more about doing some kind of crime to get put back into prison rather than drinking. Certainly, the thought of escape from reality popped up from time to time. So I told Garv that the only thing that worked for me when I got thirsty was to work with others. By this time, I had been elected the hospitals and institutions chair for our local intergroup, so I had lots of connections with different facilities around town. Garv and I started hitting a bunch of different meetings in treatment centers and detoxes, and things got a bit better — but not a whole lot. Then one day, I got a call from the coordinator of a halfway house for youth offenders. He said that no volunteers would come in anymore, because the last time they took a meeting in to the kids, the kids all started throwing the Big Books back at them. He said that it was nearly impossible to hold a meeting for these kids who were mandated by the facility to go, because they constantly acted out. He recommended that we discontinue the meeting. I told him I thought I might have someone I could bring to the meeting whom they probably wouldn't throw Big Books at, and maybe we should give it one more try.

So off to the halfway house Garv and I went. Now, I knew that none of these kids was going to mess with Garv, but I doubted that either of us was going to have much of an impact on any of these juvenile delinquents. I couldn't have been more wrong. They took to Garv like bees to honey. Acting tough around Garv just didn't make sense, and those kids knew it. He had been every place they had been and probably every place they might be going to. And he had this incredible way with them. He knew the pecking order of the kids right away and could win over the top dog in a matter of minutes. And in the cases where a kid, no way, no how, was going to go along with Garv, he could put him in his place and pretty much eliminate his influence on the rest of the group. Those kids actually started to look forward to the weekly AA meetings, because that's when Garvar was coming. He began to sponsor half the little hoodlums. The facility even gave him permission to take the kids out for meetings and movies and stuff in the evenings. He seemed to be the only one, at the time, who was really getting through to these kids, so everyone wanted him as involved with their recovery as possible.

All these developments started having an incredible effect on the rest of Garv's life. In a short amount of time, he was asked to become a live-in house president for one of the larger recovery houses in town.

He also decided that youth counseling was the direction in which he wanted to go as a career, so he applied for grants and loans and registered for college. Up until then, he had been working in manual labor jobs like roofing and landscaping because those were the only jobs he could get so soon out of prison. He figured he had nothing to lose by becoming a full-time student. He eventually started taking meetings into the lock-down treatment center attached to the youth jail in town, and the results were pretty much the same. He seemed to have the gift with any group of young men he worked with.

I tagged along with him to these different youth meetings for about eight months or so, but eventually burned out on those types of facilities. I just didn't have the patience needed for those groups of kids. But I really did enjoy watching Garv work with them. It has been one of the highlights of my sobriety.

After about a year of taking the meeting into the youth treatment facility and going to college, Garv got offered an entry-level counseling job there. And probably not more than a year later, the after-care counseling position opened up. The problem for Garv was that the position required a bachelor's degree or equivalent experience in the field. But Garv figured, what the heck, and put in for it anyway. It turned out that all the kids in the facility went into the director's office and told him that they wanted Garv to be their after-care counselor, and that was that. So here he was, just three years out of prison, with his own office, computer, and even business cards. Watching Garv hand out his business cards to some of his buddies at our home group had to be one of the prettiest sights I've ever seen. One of the neatest things about these developments with Garv was that he became a hero for the guys still locked up in Sheridan. The first thing they wanted to hear about when I showed up was the latest news on Garv. A lot of the guys could remember Garv coming into the meeting and how angry he was. Hell, he was angry even for an inmate, let alone us sweet folks on the outside. Hearing stories about him becoming a professional and working with these kids was downright inspirational. They all started thinking they had a chance to make it on the outside. I'm telling you, hope can be pretty damn contagious.

Garv is still working as a counselor, and I'm still going into facilities. I really feel like H & I work is some of the purest Twelfth-Step work out there these days. There's just not as many of those classic Twelfth-Step calls of old. Most people find out about AA and recovery through treatment facilities, psych wards, or jails these days. In facilities, you get that rare chance to talk to someone who doesn't know anything about AA and desperately wants to get sober. It is a great feeling to let them know that there is a way out.

I'm not writing just to tell you some kind of fairy tale, though. We all know that there are no guarantees that Garv or I will stay sober. We both certainly have our good days and bad. But I do know that the incredible events that we have experienced in the program can never be taken away, not even with a drink. They happened, and no one can say this thing doesn't work.

I remember my sponsor, Jack, giving me a pep talk some time ago when I was all bummed out about the progress of a sponsee I had. He told me that all you can do is tell him what worked for you. The rest is up to him and God. And every once in a while, the guy "gets it" and then you get a front-row seat to the miracle.

Harold B.
Eugene, Oregon
July 2002

A State of Honor

I only saw "Mary" three times. The first was a Wednesday evening, and I had arrived at the meeting hall early to help set up chairs and put out ashtrays. The group secretary was in the kitchen making coffee.

The door opened and a tiny, very old Indian woman made her way into the room. She looked extremely nervous. "Hi, come on in and have a seat," I said. "We'll be starting the meeting soon."

She didn't reply, just headed straight for a chair against the wall in the back of the room. She sat down, folded her hands in her lap, and looked down at the floor.

As each of our regulars came in, she was invited to join us at the table, but she shook her head no, eyes downcast.

During the meeting, Mary never looked up. She listened with rapt attention. When we joined hands for the closing prayer, she stood in reverence, but did not join the circle.

She then sat down, again hands in lap, until all members had left except for the secretary and me. Then she approached me and said, "My name is Mary. I drink too much. I can't stop. They said you understand Indians. Will you help me?"

The secretary finished her cleaning of the coffeepot and then left us to be alone for a private talk.

With tears in her eyes, Mary told how her son, a very strong middle-aged Indian man, steeped in the old way, had forbidden her to ask for help. He believed going outside the family for help would bring great shame to the family, that Indian people take care of their own. Outsiders can't help because they don't understand the old way. She wiped the tears from her brown cheeks as she said, "But I can't stop drinking. No one in the family knows how to help me stop. What can I do?"

She explained that tonight she had sneaked away from the house so her son wouldn't know, and if caught, she would be in a state of dishonor in the family. She said she could never, ever return to another meeting; she was frightened of what her son might do.

I breathed a fervent prayer that my Higher Power would give me the right things to say. And for the next hour I told Mary everything I could remember that helps a newcomer. I then went outside to the trunk of my car and got out a big paper grocery sack. From my "emergency supply" of AA literature, I put a Big Book, some pamphlets, and a copy of the Serenity Prayer into the sack.

I told Mary, "Take these things home. If your son asks, tell him you went out to get some things you need." I winked and said, "If we're lucky, he'll think you went to the grocery store for woman things. When he goes to work, read everything I've given you. My phone number is inside the cover of the Big Book, if you have questions. Try to work the program as it tells about it in the first 164 pages of the book. Meantime, we don't believe in lying, even in the tiniest form, so watch for the right time, and then tell your son where you went tonight and what was really in this sack. And tell him how the visit and the books have helped you. You may be surprised at his reaction." I told her not to worry, no one from here would give away her secret.

She went away, carrying her sack of hope. I never expected to see her again at a meeting.

However, six months later, I again arrived early at the meeting hall. Mary was waiting outside the door. She smiled and touched me on the arm and said, "I hope they call on me tonight. I want to talk."

Mary was called on to speak first. She haltingly told how she had come to that first meeting, and what I had told her to do.

She said, "I went home and did what she told me. I read all the books and every one of the pamphlets. I did my best to do what the book says, and I managed to stop drinking, one day at a time. Today my son told me he was proud of me for not drinking anymore. This looked like the right time to me, so I told my son what I had done. He was very quiet for a long time, and I was scared he would be angry, but then he said I must attend one more meeting. He said I must tell you thank you for a new life for an old woman. He told me I have brought honor to the family. I have been sober for five months."

Somehow, the closing prayer meant a great deal more to us that night as Mary placed her brown hands in ours and joined us.

I saw Mary a third time. Her picture was in the paper, two weeks after she had attended our meeting. Mary had died, peacefully, in her sleep. Sober. In a state of honor.

We sent flowers to her funeral. The card read simply, "Welcome to the best meeting of all, Mary. Save a place for us."

S. F.

Coulee Dam, Washington

March 1987

~~

Section Two

One Among Many

"Welcome" is a word not frequently heard by alcoholics, at least until they walk into an AA meeting. Once there, the sense of relief can be immediate. "Beaten into complete defeat by alcohol," writes Bill W. in a June 1958 Grapevine article, "confronted by the living proof of release, and surrounded by those who can speak to us from the heart, we have finally surrendered. And then, paradoxically, we have found ourselves in a new dimension, the real world of spirit and of faith."

Walking into an AA meeting often takes courage — and desperation. But our kinship of common suffering and the identification between one alcoholic and another provide the framework of mutual need that is the centerpiece of our group communication.

In AA, there are all kinds of groups. Some, like the one in this section from Papua, New Guinea, can be as informal as a gathering in the back seat of a car on a rainy afternoon, listening to a speaker tape. Others, more formal, may have a greeter welcoming anxious newcomers or a hospital and institutions committee extending the hand of AA into the community.

Whatever the make-up of the group, one fact remains: "Each group has but one primary purpose — to carry its message to the alcoholic who still suffers." So says AA's Tradition Five.

~

The Key to Belonging

Growing up, I was an angry, lonely, frightened kid. I didn't know how to make friends, and I wasn't sure I wanted to. Recess was the most painful part of my day — I'd sit on the outskirts of the playground, sensing that I wasn't welcome to play tag or kickball. I watched the other children, taking in their every move, and wondering if I'd ever figure it out. I started drinking heavily when I was thirteen. It wasn't to fit in — I rarely drank around other people—but more to ease the misery that was raging inside me.

It was only five years later that I arrived in the rooms of Alcoholics Anonymous. But I wasn't convinced that I wanted what you had. I did know that I didn't want to drink. I had been trying so hard to stop, and it was my failed attempts that had led me to AA. But five years of alcoholic drinking hadn't taught me how to participate in much of anything. I did show up, going to at least a meeting a day, often more; I got a sponsor (though I had no clue how to talk to her); and I didn't drink, no matter what. I sat and watched, wanting to do AA the same way I had done recess — on the outside looking in.

Ironically, I joined a group only because I wanted to be left alone. Ann seemed to be at most of the meetings I went to, and she'd zoom right in on me. "Have you joined a group yet? You could join this one!" My sponsor had also suggested I join a group, but I quickly mastered the art of sidestepping her suggestions. Ann, however, would drill me about it. "You'll drink again if you don't join a group," she'd say. I'd think, "Yeah right, I'll show you." But I figured she'd back off if I told her I'd joined a different group, and I picked one neither she nor my sponsor attended. "You're a member if you say you're a member" I'd heard, so it wasn't like I had to tell anyone other than Ann, and maybe my sponsor. Ann seemed disappointed that she hadn't roped me into one of her groups, but she moved on to another newcomer. Mission accomplished!

My sponsor, however, only suggested it wasn't good enough to simply join the group — I should "get active." She asked when the next business meeting was, and when I told her, she insisted on going with me. I was relieved when she sat quietly through the meeting. I certainly wasn't interested in making coffee or putting away chairs.

One night I went to my new home group, only to be told there was no meeting that night. The hospital needed that room for some other function, although they had made available a room in an adjoining building. My group had decided it wasn't worth lugging our gear over, so they had canceled the meeting.

I'd love to tell you that I volunteered to do the work — that I carried a coffee pot across the parking lot and went back for a box of meeting lists, pamphlets, and Big Books. But that's not what I did. I hadn't yet developed any sense of responsibility. I didn't care about the other group members, or the newcomer who might walk in the door that night. I was furious that my meeting had been canceled. I screamed at the handful of members who were directing people like me to other meetings in town that evening. Then I walked home, vowing never to go to that meeting again.

After about a year of not drinking, my defiance started to soften. My anger, my stubbornness, my attitude — these were all keeping me from enjoying my sobriety, and I started to recognize that fact. I decided to try some of the things that until then I'd refused to do. I finished my Fourth Step, and shared it with my sponsor. I started going to meetings a little early and resisted the urge to bolt out the door the moment the Lord's Prayer was finished. I thought I might try some of that "get active" stuff, so I volunteered to make coffee at a meeting I liked to attend.

You meet a lot of people when you need to be at the meeting an hour early. There's always the second person to get there — maybe a newcomer, or an out-of-towner, or even an old-timer who knows that the coffee maker needs some company. It wasn't long before I found myself in the middle of Alcoholics Anonymous. I discovered that there really is an easier, softer way — the way of striving to be a part of. What I've been willing to give to AA, most often through my home group, I've gotten back tenfold in peace of mind. Not that making coffee rendered me white as snow. The first time I was elected treasurer I stole the group's money! When the rent was due, there was nothing left to pay it with. I had to tell the group what I had done, and I vowed to pay it back, which I did. They didn't want me to be treasurer anymore (they were sober, not stupid), but found I made a good chip-person and cake baker. A few years later, in a different group, I was again asked to be treasurer, a job which I at first declined. I related the story of how I'd proven myself to be a sober thief, but they were insistent I take the job. This time I managed to perform my duties with honor and integrity.

I recently moved and now I have another new home group. I got active here immediately — I needed to. I walked into that meeting not knowing a soul and felt as if I was back at recess again. So I served as the greeter, introducing myself to these strangers I knew were just friends I hadn't met yet, and I welcomed them to the meeting. I took care of other odds and ends, such as selling raffle tickets or signing court papers and I was just elected alternate general service representative. I go on commitments with the other group members, sharing my experience, strength, and hope as a representative of the Manchester Original Group. This fall we will celebrate the group's fifty-fifth anniversary. I can't believe I'm a member of a group that's older than my mother.

I don't corner newcomers in exactly the same way that Ann did, insisting they join a group, but I think I understand what she wanted me to know. So I ask the newcomer to help me wash the coffee pot, or put chairs away, because service was, and still is, my key to belonging.

Karen S.
Manchester, New Hampshire
September 2000

༄

AA at Its Best

Each Saturday at 9:00 a.m., the small AA group in Papua, New Guinea, meets in a tiny room above the Lutheran Church administration building. We are a small group, eight members only.

Last Saturday it rained all day. Blinding sheets of water hammered down. My little station wagon ducked like a submarine through the lake-like puddles on my way to the meeting. At the meeting place, though, I found the gate locked. I thought, perhaps I'm a bit early, so I'll just wait.

The tape player in my car had a new set of batteries in it, and I happened to have a rare AA speaker tape with me, passed on to me by one of our almost nonexistent AA visitors. So, amid the pounding sheets of rain, safe in my car, I put in the tape of Clarence S., the 1973 guest speaker of an AA convention in California, and sat back to listen.

Meanwhile, Noah arrived for the meeting, barefoot and wet. I threw open the car door and he climbed in. "Listen brother," I said, "this is AA at its best." Soon Pondros arrived, also barefoot, after walking nine miles through the rain. So did Luke, Tokeso, and Kapi, but not the secretary with the key to the gate. The tape rolled on. Clarence was telling how he started the first AA group in Cleveland, Ohio in 1938. That first meeting had been literally a riot, with drunks and reporters fighting. But the meeting kept going. (I turned up the sound. With the rain drumming on the roof and all those bodies packed into the car, full volume was necessary.)

Someone, it seemed, had brought a few signs reading "Think" to the first Cleveland meetings. Said Clarence of this, "Any alcoholic coming into AA cannot think; he has nothing left to think with. The alcoholic feels, he does not think. The Third Step sorts out the men from the boys when you select a caretaker whom you trust with your will and your life. If you've done the first nine Steps of the program,

don't ask your Higher Power for another day of sobriety. You are
sober. There must be better things to ask for your needs right now!
When you pray and meditate, remember, the Lord gave you two ears
and one mouth." When you pray, Clarence said, you are talking to
God. When you meditate, you are listening.

The tape was over. The time had gone too quickly, and the secre-
tary had never come. The rain pelted down. We said the Serenity
Prayer, drove to a roadhouse, and had some coffee and a bite to eat.
What a meeting it was!

Colin C.
Papua
September 1992

♪

Fifth Tradition

Each group has but one primary purpose — to carry its message to
the alcoholic who still suffers.

On my fourth sober AA day, I was sitting alone in one of our
musty old meeting rooms, very sad and very broke. All the AAs had
seemed very kind in their desire to help, but none of them had
mentioned money. And like thousands of other new members, I
believed my biggest problems were financial. Yet not one person had
offered a loan.

Then, suddenly, one of those big, handsome, gray-templed, well-
dressed old-timers strode in with a friendly smile widening his face.
He stuck out his hand and squeezed mine. "If I can help you any way
at all, just say so, and I'll do it!" he declared heartily.

Trying to sound as if I was merely asking for a match, I said, "I
hope so. You see, I need to borrow $2,000."

His silence was total.

But finally he spoke. "You're in the wrong place," he said firmly. "We don't lend money here, my friend. That's not what this place is for."

I froze, but he went on and on. "We won't help you with a money problem. We won't help you with a family problem or a job or clothes or a medical problem or food or a place to spend the night. All we will do in AA is help you stay sober," he explained. "Then you can take care of these other problems yourself. You can take care of yourself, can't you, if you're sober?"

I hated that word "sober." But what could I say? "Certainly," I snapped, humiliated that, in my ignorance of AA folkways, I had been caught in a faux pas, as if someone had found me eating peas with my fingers.

What the man had said made perfectly good sense. I had been sober a few days and could take care of things. So I put my gradually clearing mind to it, remembered a cousin I had not tapped for months, sent a wire, and got some dough.

To my astonishment and sorrow, I almost instantly found myself drunk.

Within a few hours, my new AA benefactor had given me in very blunt words a sharp summary of Traditions Five, Six, and Seven. And by getting drunk, I had illustrated perfectly the special sense behind Five. What I needed most was not money, obviously. After getting it, I still had the drinking problem that had made me think of approaching AA in the first place.

This happened in January 1945, and the first hint of the Twelve Traditions was not to appear anywhere in AA until the July 1945 issue of the Grapevine, when Bill W. wrote, "I would like to discuss in coming issues such topics as anonymity, leadership, public relations, the use of money in AA, and the like."

Therefore, what I encountered in AA during my first few months, before the Traditions were formalized, consisted of customs of AA behavior followed by members who had learned that some AA ways would work and others would not.

That is the authority of the Traditions in my personal life. I honor them, not solely because of their authorship or their having the mystical number twelve or their being adopted by the Fellowship at the First International Convention, in Cleveland in 1950. I cherish them because they work. They enable me and my fellow AAs to stay sober, together, and to carry our message to other alcoholics.

But I did not like the Traditions at first, especially when they conflicted with what I wanted. I was a suspicious character, often turning phony operator to get what I wanted. During those first weeks, I kept wondering what "those AAs" were really up to or out after, and what I could get out of them.

The real miracle is that most of them acted with extraordinary kindness. No matter what I tried to maneuver out of them, they tried just to give me the message.

In subsequent years, I tried to misuse AA in two ways; that is, I tried to get more out of it than the sobriety message. Once, I wangled a part-time job from a fellow member, then took advantage of him. Coming in late, I would excuse myself by thinking, "After all, we're both alcoholics; he ought to excuse my little weaknesses." He exploited me, too, expecting long hours of unpaid work simply because I was a fellow AA. We began to concentrate on what we were owed, not on what we as AA owed each other. Neither of us got drunk, but our friendship did not survive.

Another time, I tried to use AA for romance, and really did find balm for a lonely heart with an AA partner. We found romance, all right, but we lost our sobriety.

Years have gone by since I had AA infancy as an excuse for my gimme tendencies. Today, I try to look at the Fifth Tradition as a giver, not as a taker. But the picture is not pretty enough to brag about. It isn't always easy, even now, to keep my personal wants out of the way when I try to carry the message. I want applause as an AA speaker, compliments as a Grapevine writer. I want to be a "success" as a sponsor — that is, I want to be the one who sobered somebody up!

I have found I prefer to carry the message to pleasant, attractive, grateful alcoholics who do what I say and give me full credit for their sobriety. Sometimes, I wish I did not even have to carry the message at all; I wish I could just wait where I am for people to come and pick it up.

On the other hand, I rejoice that I can now participate in so many good ways of fulfilling our primary purpose. I can help put on public meetings and other public-information activities to carry the message to the alcoholics who are still out there drinking, sick scared, completely unaware that we want them, and completely wrong in their notion of what our sober life is like. I can be on our hospital- and jail-visiting committees. I can serve on my group's hospitality committee, to welcome the ill-at-ease new man. I can attend or lead beginners meetings. I can help support our local intergroup office and the AA General Service Office, which reach drunks in places I cannot get to. I can have coffee with the new man after the meeting, instead of running off to chin and gossip with my old friends.

Yes, my group (made up of individual AAs, including me) has improved a lot in its respect for our Fifth Tradition — in its ways of carrying the message. My own AA history has lengthened considerably since I first caught glimpses of the sobriety-preserving wisdom in the AA ways of doing things, summed up in our Traditions. But I have recently discovered something else quite wonderful about the Fifth: It does not say that AAs should help only newcomers.

I do not agree that the newcomer is the most important member at any meeting. In my opinion, equally important are those old-timers who showed me the way, and any middle-timer who may today be suffering. If newcomers are indeed the lifeblood of AA, old- and middle-timers are its skin and backbone. What a bewildered mess we would be in without them!

So in your next meeting, when that Tradition about carrying the message "to the alcoholic who still suffers" is mentioned, please give a thought, not only to newcomers, but also to the alcoholics older in AA who are sitting there. One of them might be me. I still suffer, sometimes. I still need to hear the message, always.

B. L.

June 1970

Unity Seldom Means That We All Agree

Tradition One

Our common welfare should come first; personal recovery depends upon AA unity.

That night I left my home group business meeting in tears, after what I saw as a bitter quarrel. I was surprised to realize that what I was feeling was not anger, but fear — that this group, which had shown me love and acceptance during my first shaky weeks, might break up over minor disagreements. What would happen to me then?

Walking into the coffee shop where members of the group often met after meetings, I was startled to see those who had been most vocal in their disagreement sitting together, talking amicably, and apparently the best of friends.

Was their disagreement resolved or forgotten? Not at all. They were practicing the principles of Alcoholics Anonymous. They were placing their recovery before their personal disagreement. While they disagreed regarding what was best for the group, they were willing to allow the process of arriving at an informed group conscience to work, and then to accept that group conscience. They were able to set aside their differences while this happened and continue to care for one another and for their sobriety.

I'd like to say that I learned this lesson and was able to put it into practice immediately, but that was not the case. As usually happens, it took repetition and some sustained personal discomfort for me to learn something about unity. There inevitably came a time in my sobriety when I felt strongly about problems which I saw in my home group. Suddenly I found myself at the center of a controversy, feeling that I must defend my position and convince others that what I wanted was in the best interests of the group. After all, this was a matter of principle. I was certain that not only was my will right for me, but essential to the survival of the group (maybe even AA as a whole)!

When the group reached a decision which I believed was wrong I went through fear (what will happen to my group?), anger (how dare they do this!), guilt (I should have done more to convince them), and self-pity (they didn't vote for this because they don't like me). I wanted to run away because that had always been my response to uncomfortable emotions. But through the example of others I was able to sit still and wait.

Much to my surprise, the group didn't fail, AA as a whole didn't appear to be affected by the decision, and we all continued to stay sober. Some time later the group reversed itself and decided to change direction, handling group business in a way that I believed was more in keeping with our Twelve Traditions. Life and recovery went on and the group flourished.

What I've learned is that unity seldom means that we all agree on everything. Nor is unity served by setting aside our concerns and conforming to the majority opinion (or the vocal minority). My experience has been that unity is best achieved by a full hearing of all points of view, followed by some time for all of those involved to step back from emotional responses to the issue, as well as careful consideration and prayer for that which will best serve the group or Alcoholics Anonymous as a whole. I've also learned that when a decision is reached which doesn't work for the good of the group it can be changed. Nothing is set in stone, and we have the ability to learn from our mistakes in sobriety.

When we need to make a decision it's important for me to allow the group conscience to work and to trust in the process of applying the Twelve Traditions in making our decisions. When I'm able to do this, I feel that I'm a part of this Fellowship and that we are united in our common disease, our common solution, and our common purpose.

Mickey H.
Springville, Utah
January 1998

ॐ

The Light in the Window

Recently, a woman came to our meeting whom we hadn't seen for a while. Afterwards, she thanked us warmly for being there. The group had been her AA family that night. She had left a difficult personal situation and the meeting relieved the pain she felt. She said, "I saw the light in the window," and knew that the meeting was being held and immediately felt better.

Just an ordinary AA story. What made it different is that there were only four people in the room including herself. Once this particular group had an attendance of over twenty on a regular basis. Those who attended considered themselves members. There was never a problem in finding people to do the service work to keep the group going. Then attendance started to thin out. It was a gradual process. The usual suspects — inevitable deaths, new jobs, moving away, going to different meetings — all contributed.

Regular attendance dwindled to ten and then lower. Those attending were still strong in their AA program, many with lengthy sobriety. They were able to share and listen to sharing. When meetings saw only five or six around the table, the group conscience was taken to see whether the group should be kept going. Maybe the energy and funds that the few remaining members were putting into the upkeep of the group might be used to better AA purpose.

But the decision was always to keep meeting, no matter how few attended. Not very rational thinking in the outside world but perfectly normal in AA. It was important to keep the meeting going for the few who considered themselves members and were regular in their attendance. They were drunks who needed the experience, strength, and hope they received every week to keep their sobriety alive.

There was more than their own sobriety at stake. They knew that a major tool in the AA program was spreading the message. Always there was the thought that "whenever anyone reaches out. . . the hand of AA should be there." The woman who was so relieved to find the group active was not the first who saw "the light in the window," showing that the group was still offering the hand of AA. In the past it had happened enough for the group to know that the light was important.

My home group is not the only local one experiencing loss of membership. There are six to eight groups in a two-mile radius that are suffering the same losses. At first the situation seems temporary (because of people going on vacation or the like), but gradually it becomes apparent that the losses may be permanent.

Is it only in one community that some AA groups are dwindling? Personal experience shows that this is not a unique experience. While traveling, it is often important to get to a meeting. A call to the intergroup in an area gives the name and address of a meeting that night. Often you get to one that is vibrant and alive with many in attendance. But often there are only five or six people there. Talking with the members shows the same pattern as in my home group. Attendance has fallen off and there is a constant struggle to keep going.

There seems to be no easy answer to this problem. It is not for personal pride that those in a small group keep the group going; they want AA to be available. But there is always the thought that we are not self-supporting because the institution that lets us use their space for the meeting is gracious enough to lower or waive the already low rent. Can this really be in accord with the Seventh Tradition?

It wouldn't be fair to see this as a failure of AA in the area: other older groups still flourish, and new ones spring up and grow. Still, some think that not enough has been done to follow the AA guidelines when a group starts to lose members. I've heard the remaining members accused of not working their program properly or enough. There is no question that members of an AA group can display many of the habits that cause failure in the outside world. "We are not saints."

I was once involved in starting a group. Like-minded people, all experienced in AA, thought they saw a need. The day and time selected didn't compete with other groups, a coffee pot was obtained, and a hall was rented. At first everything went well. The group flourished and gradually grew. But during the second year, it was seen that fewer people were attending. The enthusiasm of the founders dwindled as personal problems came up. Finally in the third year, with almost no attendance, it was decided to close the group.

Those who made the decision thought it was the will of God. Perhaps they missed the slogan "Pray As If Everything Depended on God, Work As If Everything Depends on Ourselves." Sobriety can be endangered when we fail to reach out and continue to reach out.

Can we account for the lessening of group participation seen in many places? Is it a recent phenomenon? It is noticeable that some people come to a meeting just as it starts and go out the door as soon as it is over. They are there for the meeting and not for the group.

These minimal givers don't realize that the group is the basic building block of the program. It isn't important whether the lack of interest in the group is attributed to the increased demands on people's time or because many attendees come from treatment programs where they learn about AA from a nongroup perspective. What is important is that without vital groups, there can be no place to practice the program. It isn't possible for all of us to be loners.

Meanwhile, what about my home group? The members still keep "the light in the window." Individuals still come in and express thanks that the group is still there. Recently there were ten people in attendance. In order to maintain sobriety, both for members and anyone who comes by, the group will continue, praying only to know God's will and to have the power to carry it out.

Anonymous
Lake Worth, Florida
June 1999

~~

What Meeting Are You Going to Tomorrow?

When the sheriff came to help my terrified wife grab a few of her belongings from our house so she could leave me, I was passed out in a drunken stupor on the bed. That day I had drunk more than I had in the decade we'd been together. I turned into an insane, infantile, terrorizing, and abusive beast that last day of drinking. I'm sure I had come close before but I was in rare form that day. It culminated with me trying to wrench a set of car keys out of her hand. She was gripping them too tightly for my liking, so I bit her arm with vigor. She screamed and called for the police, and I made a cowardly escape, bribing some stranger at an ATM for a quick ride out of Forestville to avoid arrest.

I threw up for four hours the next morning. Back at my house, I barely noticed that anything was missing. Her toothbrush? Hair brush? Where was she? She was gone. I lay down in the throbbing of my misery and wished to die. This is where the first of the prayers went up. In the past, all of my prayers had been the barter variety: "Get me out of this situation and I'll be a good boy forever and ever, amen." This one was much more simple and I meant it with all my heart: "God, please help me."

I was alone on the floor of my house for three days. I drank only water. I was terrified to leave for fear of drinking. Finally I called the AA hotline and learned that there was a meeting in Graton on Thursday night. I had visited three AA meetings back in 1992, just long enough to learn that I wasn't one of them and could get on with my drinking. It was now May of 1998, and I waited for the meeting secretary to ask if there were any newcomers. He did. I said, "My name is Chris and I'm an alcoholic." A trickle of tears became a river then. I let go. I was tired of fighting it and I let go.

The tears didn't stop throughout that meeting. During the discussion part of the meeting, one goodlooking and nicely dressed lady motioned to me and said to the group, "He's why we're here. He's here to remind me where I came from. I've left that misery." In that moment I knew they had all been where I was; I didn't have any words for this place. They did. They called it "pitiful, incomprehensible demoralization."

After that meeting, a stranger walked over to me and put his arm across my shoulders and kindly asked, "How are you doing?" It was a moment of kindness I had not expected. I knew I was the scum of the earth. I had wounded my wife and she had left me and I was alone and jobless and didn't know what to do. We talked for a while and what I remember him saying as he gave me his business card is this, "You hang in there. Take it one day at a time and call me if you need to talk to someone." I felt like I existed. I felt like I was cared for. His name was David and today he's my sponsor.

I went to the Friday night Occidental meeting the next day. At the end of that meeting, I was still in a fog. Two clean-cut guys about my age, late twenties or early thirties I guessed, came up to me and started asking questions. "How many days sober are you?" "How is it going?" "Feeling better?" I didn't have any time to dwell on the fact that I had lost the love of my life and my prospects were pitiful. This was Matt and Aaron. They held out their hands to me and pulled me into the boat of AA. And Aaron asked me what I believe is the most important question a newcomer needs to be asked during his first few weeks of sobriety, "Where are you going tomorrow?"

"What do you mean?" I asked back.

"What meeting are you going to tomorrow?" he clarified.

"Oh, I didn't know there was a meeting tomorrow," I said.

Aaron laughed and put a meeting schedule in my hand. I am fortunate to live in a county that has many different meetings each and every day. Aaron stood next to me and circled all the meetings that he found worked for him. He was still concerned about where I was going to go tomorrow and he said, "Saturday night, Forestville. It's a great meeting. I'll see you there."

I went. Aaron was there. So were a bunch of the same people I had seen in Graton, and Occidental the two previous nights. I had already heard the drill: read the Big Book, go to meetings, get a sponsor, and work the Steps, and if you are serious, go to ninety meetings in ninety days. I was nothing but serious and the fact that these same faces were showing up at meetings each and every day made me feel all right going to meetings each and every day. During my first ninety days, I usually went to both a morning meeting and an evening meeting.

At meetings they said, "Grab the phone list and call someone if you start craving a drink or if you get lonely." This seemed like about the stupidest thing in the world to me. How could I possibly call a stranger? I'm a real man. I don't need help from other people. They had a word for this kind of thinking: stinking. So I called people on the phone list. Strangers. They were kind to me. I called Matt. Kind.

Aaron. Kind. Maria. Kind. Each conversation ended with, "I'll see you at the meeting."

I had a particularly grueling day just a couple months into sobriety. They had all promised that things would start to get better. Well, it wasn't happening for me! There was this guy named Tim fixing his coffee next to me right before the Tuesday night meeting in Sebastopol. He had always seemed kind of aloof to me and I had avoided him. He asked me, "How are you doing?"

I answered, "Pretty poorly. When does it start to get better?"

"It does get better," he said.

He went and sat down to lead the meeting. When his harrowing share was complete, he said this to the group, "Someone just asked me a really good question: when does it start to get better? That's what I'd like to hear about tonight."

When my concern that day became the topic of that meeting I felt like I went from being a sober visitor to AA meetings to being a member of AA. I stood with Tim outside that meeting and thanked him for doing that.

I meet Tim at a lot of meetings now, and I always stay after and talk with him. He has helped me through the darkest periods of sobriety. We talked about the restraining order my wife brought against me. We talked about the hearing. We talked about the two telephone conversations when she insisted that divorce was the only course of action. Tim always said, "Just listen to her."

I whined about the pain of her leaving me. I whined to David, to Tim, to Matt, to any AA that would stand still long enough for me to rip from my pocket one of the printed-out E-mails she had sent me. Invariably, all my AA friends told me, "Don't do anything. Just listen."

I didn't do anything. I just listened. When I started listening to my wife, our conversations started to get better. (Imagine that.) When I started listening to my wife, I was amazed by all she had to say. The more I listened to my wife the better things got. Now I get to listen to her in a new house that we are sharing as equal partners in a completely new marriage to each other. Our separation lasted over eight months. She began to work the Al-Anon program during those eight months and we suddenly have more in common than ever: faith in a Higher Power and prayer. We read AA and Al-Anon literature to one another. We pray and meditate together. We are both profoundly grateful for the lessons about God, communication, and recovery that we have learned in the rooms of AA and Al-Anon.

My life has improved so much since that last awful day of drinking that I am truly amazed before I am halfway through. My recovery relies on the hands of many people being extended to me. The welcome I received was more than a word. It was a word followed by actions. I am never alone in AA. I have played tennis with alcoholics. Had many lunches and dinners with AAs. Gone on drives to forests and beaches with AAs. AAs, especially my sponsor, have helped me many times. They have helped me move. Helped me fix my car.

And most importantly they have taught me to pray. When I go to meetings and see tough, world-ravaged men and women turning their lives over to the care of a Higher Power, I am reminded that God is my director.

This is the Alcoholics Anonymous that helped me rebuild my life after I had torn it down with booze. This is the Alcoholics Anonymous that I owe to each trembling and shaky-footed newcomer who gets fed up with his life enough to look for something new.

Chris R.
Santa Rosa, California
November 1999

⤳

Section Three

Working with Others

The impact one alcoholic can have on the life of another is profound. And it doesn't take any special skills to accomplish — all it takes is the willingness to communicate with one another in the language of the heart.

From the university professor in this section who sponsored hundreds in his community to the shy woman working as an intergroup volunteer, taking responsibility for the well-being of others has resulted in changed lives — their own and those they reached out to.

As Bill W. points out in his essay on Tradition Five from the September 1952 Grapevine, reprinted in the "Twelve and Twelve":

"The unique ability of each AA to identify himself with, and bring recovery to, the newcomer in no way depends upon his learning, eloquence, or on any special individual skills. The only thing that matters is that he is an alcoholic who has found a key to sobriety. These legacies of suffering and of recovery are easily passed among alcoholics, one to the other. This is our gift from God, and its bestowal upon others like us is the one aim that today animates AAs all around the globe."

⤳

The Hands of AA

I have watched alcoholics' hands for over thirty years. Hands drinking. Newcomers' hands. Sober sponsors' hands. The hands of AA. God's hands.

For fifteen years my hands had a death grip on the neck of a booze bottle. I never reached the point of having to use a towel around my neck to get a drink up to my mouth without spilling it (I wasn't that bad), but I do remember my first day without a drink in my hand, mimicking Dr. Strangelove, reaching into the cupboard for a nonexistent bottle. "Stop that!" I told my hand, slapping it.

For years each day began with a drink in hand, then a cigarette and coffee. Each night my hands wrung each other in a prayer to God not to let me die during the night, followed immediately with a futile promise that tomorrow would be different. Then came the regular nightcap and off to my nightmares.

The teaching and newspaper jobs disappeared in boozy firings and resignations after about ten years and I entered my "handout" phase. My hand was always out for a free drink or a loan. Married, with three small children, I ripped off their piggy banks. When my wife left with the children, she took the car too. I trained my thumb to look really sad and persecuted. I thumbed a lot of rides to the nearest bar. As a top reporter and editor, I had met a lot of important people around the Ohio Valley. Now they no longer offered their hands in greeting.

Still, I thought I could "handle" things. When the gas company turned off the heat in the middle of winter, my hands got very cold. Alone in that house, miles from the nearest neighbor, I talked to myself all day long. My hands clenched into fists of rage, my index finger loaded and aimed and pointing to the former bosses, friends, and family who had handed me the pink slips of rejection, the legal papers of divorce, the written (I had no phone) refusals for further loans.

I ended up empty-handed. Spiritually zero. Financially bankrupt. Family and friends missing. Worst of all, just one bottle left for my hands.

That's when Wade showed up. Insurance salesman in a big Cadillac. Just what I needed. Ha! He strode up the lawn, put out this ham of a hand, and said: "Hi, I'm Wade and I understand you have a problem and if you don't want to talk about it, we'll just shake hands and part as friends." He didn't say "alcohol" or "Alcoholics Anonymous" but I intuitively knew exactly what he meant. We shook hands. I'll never forget that touch. I connected with humanity again in that handshake. I connected with God again without knowing it. Spiritual serendipity. The loneliness of the alcoholic begins to fade when two hands connect. I still can't describe that first handshake, but without it, I wouldn't be here today.

Wade took me to my first AA meeting that night where an old political enemy I had blasted in newspaper headlines smiled, shook hands, and said: "It's about time you got here!" Lots of friendly strangers shook my hand in welcome that night. It felt like I was running for political office.

As a newcomer, my hands began to recover. After spilling a half dozen cups of coffee my first six months, I understood why the old-timers gave us new people only half a cup. I sat on my hands while nerve endings came alive. I tore styrofoam cups to shreds and contemplated the pile of pieces that resembled my powerless, unmanageable life. After ninety-two days dry, I decided to take a drink. This additional research on alcoholism lasted for thirty days. At the end of this period, I remember dialing the AA phone number three times before my stupid fingers got it right.

Anyhow, I made it back. An old-timer suggested I shake hands with everyone at the meeting. I still do that. Ever shake hands with one of your resentments? In West Virginia, we have a high percentage of coal miners and military veterans who have lost their hands. Ever shake hands with someone who doesn't have a right hand? These sober days my hands are clean. I write for a living. Some meetings I leave with dirty hands, hands wonderfully dirty with the oil of a recovering mechanic, the mud of a struggling construction worker, with the grime of honest labor.

Three stories stick out. An old man, smelling, bundled in dirty overcoat, scarf, hat over ears, dark glasses, shows up at an AA meeting. Everyone gives him a wide berth, like he's a skunk with the plague. The twisted top of a paper bag (with bottle inside) sticks out of his pocket. The meeting starts. The old man jumps up, pulls off cap and glasses. It's home group member Jack in disguise! He looks around the room and says: "No one shook my hand!" He sits down in silence.

Saturday one o'clock meeting. Across the table from me, a young overweight woman with "love" and "hate" tattooed across her knuckles is at her first AA meeting and is wringing her hands terribly. The chairman, behind those terrible one-way sunglasses, makes a biting remark about druggies and tattoos. Her hands shoot under the table. Her eyes fall and she doesn't look up again. I've never seen her again at an AA meeting. I didn't have a chance to talk to her and apologize for that guy's "sarcasm."

And this last one, a month ago at a clubhouse in Cincinnati after a meeting. Young man, unshaven, dirty, fumbling with a cup of coffee, head bowed, lips perceptibly moving as he talked to himself, totally alone in a jam-packed room of AAs, across the table from me, two chairs down. Crowded, awkward to reach him. I shake hands with the others at the table, extend my hand to him, "Hi!" He doesn't look up. He is the most confused member in the clubhouse. He is hurting the most. He is at the deepest bottom, totally lost in himself, unconnected, alone in the Fellowship. I pray. God, I can't force him to shake hands. I stand, ready to leave. He jumps to his feet, smiles weakly, and shakes my hand. I almost cried on the spot. I realized I needed his hand just as much as he needed mine.

At the end of "How It Works," we read "I am responsible. When anyone, anywhere, reaches out for help, I want the hand of AA always to be there. And for that: I am responsible." I'm going to continue watching hands . . . and shaking them.

Anonymous
Wheeling, West Virginia
October 1991

What I Learned From My Sponsor

I will never forget what my sponsor, Mark, told me the first time that we sat down to do the Steps. He told me the story of Bill W. and Dr. Bob and their first meeting. He also told me that he was taking me through the Steps in order to stay sober himself. Then he told me something that really blew my mind. He told me that someday I, too, would take other people through the Steps if I wanted to stay sober myself. With only a couple of days sober, all I could hope was that I wouldn't drink that night after I left our meeting. Carrying the message never entered my mind. I just didn't want to drink.

Mark always told me that AA was a participation in other people's lives and why that made such a profound impact on me, I don't know, but it did. So I attended meetings on a regular basis and got involved with the people in my group. Not only did I get to know them, but they got to know me. Before long, my sponsor was telling me it was time that I start sponsoring other people. He told me that getting out of myself and helping other alcoholics would help make the tough times that I was going through a little easier. Though I didn't understand that, I talked to newcomers, participated in meetings, and just made myself available, to the best of my ability.

Eventually I started sponsoring. I helped a guy or two, but he didn't stay sober. I did everything that my sponsor had done with me, but every guy I sponsored got drunk. So in frustration, I went to Mark and told him that I thought I was a lousy sponsor because all the guys I was trying to help were not recovering. He asked me a few questions, like whether I used the literature, talked about Steps, shared my experience, and so forth. I said yes. Then he got this strange look on his face and asked me if I had gotten drunk. I said no, feeling a little offended by his question. Then Mark said, "Then you might be a good sponsor." He told me the reason we try to carry the message is so that we stay sober. If the person we are helping stays sober, that's an extra bonus. So I didn't take it so personally when the people I was helping got drunk. I went on to the next one to see if I could be of some help.

My first few years of recovery were filled with a lot of changes. I got into a relationship, it ended, I went to college and graduated, I got a job, I got laid off, I broke my leg when I had no insurance, I moved, and I got my feelings hurt more than I would like to admit. When I shared with Mark some of the stuff I was going through, he listened and then asked if I was sponsoring anybody. If I said no, he told me to find someone. If I said yes, he told me to check on them or find someone else to help as well. He suggested that I might also read the bottom of page 14 and the top of page 15 in the Big Book. I would say okay and take his advice, and by taking action, always felt better.

Then in September 1999, the unthinkable happened. My father had a heart attack and went into a coma. Later in the week, he was taken off life-support. While I was sitting with my father during his last living hours, I received a phone call from a friend who was calling to check on me. I had asked him to get in touch with my sponsor, and within the hour, Mark was with me. We sat and talked, prayed, and said good-bye to my father. Later that night, I received a phone call that my father had passed away. After the funeral, I went back to the city in which I was living and went straight to an AA meeting. I had only been living there a little while, but I'd known, when I'd moved there, exactly what to do: I went to meetings early and I stayed late. I made friends, and got in touch with the person at the local intergroup. He helped me get involved in many AA projects. Before long, I was sponsoring people there, too. With all the things I was going through after losing my father, helping another alcoholic achieve sobriety helped me get through that.

I have since moved to another city, and now I sponsor new guys here. Recently, one of my sponsees lost a parent, and I was able to help him get through it as my sponsor had helped me, by telling him to make himself available to help others recover from alcoholism.

Vinny B.
Austin, Texas
May 2003

へん

An Unlikely Hero

My father passed away this year, just two months before he would have celebrated thirty years in AA. As we cleared away his desk littered with stacks of Grapevines, notes for AA meetings, and dozens of Serenity Prayers, I am painfully saddened that he didn't live to celebrate this milestone.

Up until the day he died, my father attended three meetings a week. Over the past three decades, he sponsored hundreds of people in our community.

After the wake, we retired to our family home, my brothers, sisters, and I with my mother and a few cousins and friends. I sat outside under the apple tree with my brothers, soaking in the unusually warm October air. We planted that tree when we were children, and at the time it was no bigger than ourselves. Now it towered over the house and spread over the entire backyard like a protective umbrella.

That night, we met many of the first names we had gotten to know over the telephone. We grew up accustomed to phone calls in the middle of the night and to my father's abrupt departures to attend to one of his sponsees. My father would drive ninety miles at one o'clock in the morning to take someone to a drying-out facility. So I always knew who he was and what he did, but the full impact of my father's life's work in AA didn't hit me until I met the hundreds of people whose lives had changed because of it.

Growing up, I had a love-hate relationship with Alcoholics Anonymous. My father had stopped drinking when I was nine, and I was too young to understand much of what had gone on in our chaotic household. As a university professor, he was a highly functional alcoholic. What had the most effect on me were his absences when he binged, as well as the pressure on my mother, who raised eight children more or less on her own.

But I felt his absences more keenly when he joined AA, clinging to it like the lifeline it was, and later on, dedicating his life to helping others stay sober. For much of my youth, I resented AA, not only for taking my father away from me, but for changing him.

When I became politically active as a young adult, I often met people who described snippets of my father's social activism before he joined AA. He was involved in numerous just causes, all of which he gave up when he joined AA. And although I understood that AA kept him sober, I never understood why he gave up working for social justice when he gave up alcohol.

Then, as I went through his papers in the weeks after he died, I was bowled over by the extent of his activism. I found articles he wrote in the early fifties arguing for a just "living wage" in the postwar era. A newspaper clipping from the early sixties recounted how he organized a campaign among teachers to protest the appointment of a public school superintendent perceived as racist and "unacceptable" to the minority population the system served. In the early sixties,

both my parents also had been active in setting up anti-racist committees in the newly built suburb where they lived. While he drank, he
had fought against McCarthyism, and had sat, as an economics
teacher in a Catholic university, on dozens of boards and committees.

In some ways, it was a joy to rediscover my father. Reading about
his work almost meant more after his death, because if I had asked
him about it he would have brushed it off casually or summed it up in
a few minutes, giving me the impression that everything he did before
AA was unimportant.

I felt that AA had become his life, and I resented the fact that his
involvement snuffed out so much of the important work he had done,
even though I respected him for helping people stay sober. He bailed
them out of jail, out of bars, out of hell. Drunks were deposited at our
door by police and even their own relatives, puking and crying. They
jumped off bridges, only to recover, asking for him.

Some of them we grew close to, and they became part of our family. Many others we never knew; they remained first names on the
telephone. But my father suffered with them, and I often marveled at
the fact that we, his own children, never caused him as much grief, as
much trouble, as much pain as his AA sponsees. I looked up to my
father, but I sometimes felt a confused envy. He had a bond with
them, and I feared they knew him better than I, his own daughter.

About ten years ago, at my youngest sister's graduation party, Jim
J. called from a bar seven miles away. My father brought him home
and put him in the basement to sleep it off. Unfortunately, Jim J.
decided he wasn't ready to sleep it off and kept emerging, covered
with filth and urine, clutching a thirty-dollar bottle of champagne
meant for my sister's friends. I couldn't help thinking of the mad-
woman in Jane Eyre's attic as my sisters and I vaulted fences, coolers,
and partygoers to catch Jim as he stumbled down the street in search
of alcohol. "He's our cousin," we explained in embarrassment to our
astonished friends when my father guided him back to the basement.

Several hours later, my father drove Jim to a treatment center one hundred miles away. I still can see him in my mind's eye, leading Jim away by the arm. Jim stumbles, his six-foot frame towering over my seventy-year-old father who steadies him. My father is an unlikely looking hero, his polyester pants bunched above his walking shoes. But I am struck by his droopy-drawered dignity and assuredness.

When he returned, my sister walked into the kitchen to see my dad looking despondent, defeated. Alarmed, she asked him what was wrong. "I saw a six-pack on the stairs, and suddenly I wanted a beer really badly," he told her.

After so many years, I took his sobriety for granted, and I think after that I understood him more. It was difficult having to share my father with the world, but eventually I learned to give up my resentment. AA was his lifeline, and he in turn gave more to the world as a recovering alcoholic than he did in all his years of political activism.

At the wake, I saw dozens of young men walk trembling up to the casket, wiping their eyes. They were usually alone, and they looked more shook up than I felt. Sometimes they would approach the family in the receiving line hesitantly, even reluctantly. "Your father saved my life," they'd say, voices quivering.

I heard over and over the line spoken as simple truth: "Your father saved my life." If I had any lingering resentments over my father's dedication to AA, they disappeared as I watched his life's work pass by.

The other day I took my young son to the swimming pool and taught him how to bounce up and down keeping his little chin above water. As a child, I had spent many summers at Lake Michigan with my family. Every year my father would point out the sandbar to me: "See that light patch of water?" Then we would walk out to it, and when it got too deep, he would hold my hand while I bounced up and down keeping my mouth closed to keep out the water. Suddenly, I would hit solid ground, and he'd let go of my hand so I could walk with delight on my own. I loved being that far out into the lake, looking back at the shore and seeing the distance I had come.

At the wake, I spied a young man standing in the back with his wife and baby. As he approached the casket, I was struck by his serene sadness. Though his grief was obvious, I sensed a strength in him, deeply rooted.

Later I learned his identity: he was one of the first names I remembered on the other end of the telephone. Eight years ago, his car struck and killed an eight-year-old. He was twenty years old and stone sober at the time of the tragedy, and his recovery had been difficult enough before the accident.

I remembered that turmoil — and how my father had grieved for him as he would his own son. He stuck by him, and Tommy pulled through. Seeing Tommy with his young family, his serious but steady grief, I understood my father's life in a fullness I had never thought possible.

Hannah H.
Chicago, Illinois
January 2001

&

Responsibility (Noun): The Ability to Respond

I left my first AA meeting with a pile of pamphlets handed to me by someone who I thought then was an overzealous convert, and I could not help but notice the words "I am responsible . . . " printed on several of them. As I continued to come around, I began to hear those words used often at meetings by speakers who were describing what they had become as a result of not drinking and of following the AA way of life.

Being a typical alcoholic, I naturally more than disliked the word "responsibility" and all its derivatives, as I understood its meaning and implication. To me, responsibility strictly meant obligation. And obligation, or the avoidance of it, during my years of active alcoholism, had set the pattern of my drinking. So, even though these fellows saying they had become responsible said it with unmistakable enthusiasm and gratitude in their voices, I fell back somewhat belligerently on other words, from the AA Preamble: "The only requirement for membership is a desire to stop drinking." My choice was a personal defense against something I had drunk half my life to escape.

That was some twenty-four hours ago, and living sober one day at a time transforms the alcoholic outlook. Personal beliefs and convictions based upon preconceived ideas and prejudices, the self-centered stinking thinking of the drinking days, gradually give way to those wholesome ideas that are the wisdom of the Fellowship, spiritually grounded in the Twelve Steps.

Today, responsibility no longer means what it once meant to me, a sorrow-sick alcoholic, frightened and alone. Gratefully, I have come to understand that this word defines the essential quality of sober alcoholics' lives.

Responsibility, when broken down — response-ability—means simply the ability to respond. As active alcoholics, we had the ability only to react to everything and everyone around us. We drank to remove ourselves from a world that we were powerless over, that we could not manage. In a sense, we drank to destroy our circumstances — to wipe them out of our consciousness—and ended up nearly destroying ourselves. Such is the madness of our insidious disease. But through the Fellowship of Alcoholics Anonymous and the spiritual way of recovery that is its suggested program, the madness ceases, and we are restored to sanity.

No longer viewed through blood-red eyes of guilt-ridden anger, regret, and remorse, the nightmare world ends; and we awaken to a world seen within the infinitely broader context of a Higher Power, God as we understand him. And it is from this decision to turn our will and our lives over to the care of God that the other Steps of our recovery follow.

As we strive for spiritual progress through the program, its principles show themselves more and more as invaluable methods of perceiving and meeting the needs of each day as it unfolds. No longer relying on the unreliable, i.e., our own personal ability to figure things out and manipulate them to conform to our own selfish wishes, we now simply turn to God, seeking only "knowledge of his will for us and the power to carry that out." Gradually, although at times almost miraculously, problems that once would have plagued us apparently work themselves out; burdens that once would have crushed us seem easily lifted; and obligations that at one time we would have shunned are accepted with calmness and confidence. And at last, we realize that somehow, somewhere along the way, we have been given the ability to respond — responsibility — to ourselves, to our fellow alcoholics, to our neighbor, to God, to all life's situations, to life itself.

Responsibility is a gift; and although we are not obliged to receive it, we will never come to know the peace, assurance, and love of a vital sobriety until we do. The very spirit that sustains and perpetuates our Fellowship of Alcoholics Anonymous is responsibility: each recovering alcoholic coming to affirm, "I am responsible . . . "

R. H.
Bronx, New York
September 1983

~

No More Shame

Today I spoke with a Catholic priest who in the course of his work encounters women who have a problem with alcohol. I wanted to enlist his help in spreading the word that there is a place to go if you are a woman who "habla español," who thinks that she may have a drinking problem. He told me that the number of women who need help is great and that he'll do all that he can because he knows that women are afraid to seek help "because of the shame." He and I share a frustration in knowing that these women are hard to reach. The hopelessness and shame that these women feel in admitting that there is a problem with alcohol is so great that many die without ever knowing that there is a solution to their alcoholism. At times, they are protected by well-intentioned family members, who have no idea what can be done or where they can go. Or they are told that they will be ostracized if they go "outside" the family to seek help.

While Spanish-speaking AA meetings have been available for a long time, they are usually attended by men. The sober alcoholic woman is a rarity at these meetings. It is not that my brother alcoholics are uncaring or do not welcome us. It is our fear of what people will think that keeps us from seeking help. A woman who is drunk is equated with a woman of the streets. Many in our culture do not understand that alcoholism is a disease, not a moral dilemma or a weakness.

Now there is a place where answers can be found and a woman can get on the path to sobriety. Every Tuesday night in my area, there is an Alcoholics Anonymous meeting for Spanish-speaking women. There you will find other women who are recovering from the disease of alcoholism. If you are a woman who thinks that she may have a drinking problem, come and listen. Hear the experience, strength, and hope of women just like you who are recovering from alcoholism. You can find the support you need to live a sober life, one day at a time.

Nikki S.
Rancho Cucamonga, California
September 1995

◌

Solutions Not Sadness

The first time I walked into an AA meeting I'd been ordered to do so by the court. Actually, I didn't walk — I was wheeled. I'd spent the previous four months in a hospital because of a blackout and collision with a utility pole. I was sent home with crutches, but the doctors were dubious that I'd ever walk again. I'd crushed my hip and left leg. I had hundreds of stitches all over my body, and my right eye was damaged from a blow to my head. After four months of morphine and self-pity, I wasn't in real good shape when I wheeled into AA back in 1974.

I remember the room and that my mom went with me. I remember also my total lack of understanding that I was an alcoholic. I went to those meetings and even enjoyed some of them. I volunteered at a small office AA had and did some office work there. What I didn't do for one moment was look at my accident and recognize that I was an alcoholic and my drinking had condemned me to a lifetime of pain.

For years after those first AA meetings, if you asked me what happened to me, I'd give you one of two stories about my accident. If I didn't know you, I'd tell you that a drunk ran a red light and hit me. Kind of true, don't you think? If I knew you, I'd tell you that someone drugged me. That I'd only had three drinks and that someone did this terrible thing to me. Either answer got me pity and sympathy — two emotions I learned to settle for instead of respect.

I was twenty-six years old when my car crashed into that utility pole. At that time I was using alcohol to dull the pain of living. When I reentered AA seven years later, in May 1981, I was a legal drug addict as well as a primary alcoholic. I'd had six surgeries and I suffered from depression.

A doctor was my drug connection and I couldn't survive without the pain medicines he supplied. I used Valium on a daily basis and my body looked like a railroad track. I had lots of real problems that, when X-rayed, could get me a prescription from most doctors — unless I went to the same doctor for too long, then he sometimes became suspicious. So I just kept seeing new doctors. From the outside, I looked like a middle-class handicapped woman. I looked like Suzie Cream Cheese on the outside and felt inside like a skid row bum.

When I came back to AA in 1981, God removed my desire for alcohol right away. The drugs were much harder to stop obsessing over. I was told by my sponsor to read "Doctor, Alcoholic, Addict*" from the Big Book daily for the first couple of years. I also had to experience two major surgeries along the way. I ended up with a hip replacement and total knee replacement in early recovery. The women in AA were right there for me, supporting me, and helping me through it. I depended on God instead of a drug for the first time in my life.

By the time I had a few years in AA, I was working with women who had alcoholism and another illness. I helped them to learn how to live one day at a time, using the Steps and prayer to help with their pain level. I helped them learn alternative ways to deal with pain, like exercise and holistic medicine.

For the first time in my life I began to realize that my accident was my biggest asset. I started to see the Promises come true in my life, and it felt good to have a purpose and help other women like myself. I have found it to be a real challenge.

When I was nine years sober, I began to have problems with balance, problems concentrating, and exhaustion daily. After many tests I was diagnosed with multiple sclerosis. This is an autoimmune disease that affects the nerves and muscles. It has the possibility of totally paralyzing me and can be fatal. I wish I could tell you I took the news well. I didn't. I was angry and had several days of having to go to lots of meetings because I couldn't see any other solution besides drinking again. I ran out of choices for a while, which I admitted at meetings. I prayed daily, and the terror and rage I felt passed fairly quickly.

As a result of my diagnosis and sharing it in meetings, I helped begin a woman's support group within AA. We all have had some major illness as well as alcoholism. We used God, meditation, and weekly meetings to help each other accept and move past our illnesses. These life-saving days totally changed my life. All because of AA and a terrible illness!

I'm doing quite well today. I have good days and not so good. I sponsor women, I am happily married, and I share my experience, strength, and hope on a daily basis. I cannot tell you I am happy that I have so many physical problems. If I could wish it away, I would. What I am grateful for is this beautiful Fellowship that allows me to be free of self-pity and drug dependency as well as alcoholism. I'm grateful to the women I've grown to love and been allowed to help.

I have no idea how anyone survives a serious illness without God's help. I found God's help in AA. That is a lot more powerful to me than any drink or drug I ever crawled to.

Susan L.
Carson City, Nevada
February 2000

This story was retitled "Acceptance Was the Key" in the Fourth Edition of the Big Book.

∽

〜

Section Four

Being Friendly with Our Friends

Treating alcoholics isn't necessarily the most appealing task in the world, yet there are a host of doctors, psychiatrists, members of the clergy and others who have devoted their lives to doing just that — helping alcoholics to recover. Alcoholism is a cunning, baffling, and powerful disease and the effects it has on individuals and on society as a whole are widespread and devastating.

But AA has always had any number of friends, professional men and women, who know and love AA and want to help us. We need to let them. As Bill W. noted in the March 1958 Grapevine, "More and more we regard all who labor in the total field of alcoholism as our companions on a march from darkness into light. We see that we can accomplish together what we could never accomplish in separation and in rivalry."

◡

Alcoholism and Alcoholics Anonymous

For many years, individual physicians have considered alcoholism a disease and tried to convince their colleagues and the public that alcoholics require treatment rather than punishment. It was AA that proved alcoholics could recover. And when the success of AA had been demonstrated, a great deal more interest was generated on the part of the medical profession. A great step was taken toward a possible breakthrough when, in 1956, the American Medical Association officially recognized alcoholism as an illness.

AA's approach to the illness is spiritual, and I know from experience that the spiritual attitude of a patient is of extreme importance in any illness. When I have a patient without faith, I know his chances for recovery are diminished. Faith can and does modify the actual physiology of the body.

But what about those without faith? Does this mean that AA has no place in their lives? Not at all. It does mean that AA alone may not be enough. Cooperation among all agencies interested in treating alcoholism is important. Each has its place, but each must recognize that it may not have all the answers. A combination of all facilities available offers the best approach. And with this, most AAs agree.

There is, however, a vocal minority in AA that claims AA alone can help the alcoholic. To the physician who has spent years studying and treating successfully illnesses from which he has not suffered, this cliche seems preposterous.

Some physicians refuse to treat alcoholics, and some have no understanding of the illness. We may not judge all by the few. Just as we are trying to teach all physicians that alcoholics are sick people, there should be an attempt made to teach all AA members that medicine and psychiatry also can help people suffering from the illness.

AA has a far greater responsibility than is generally recognized, even by many of its members; but this is an obligation which, if carried out, will greatly enhance the stature of the Fellowship and benefit its members immeasurably, as well. Anyone who has studied the Twelve Steps carefully knows that, in order to live the program, one must do a great deal more than maintain abstinence.

As I circulate among recovered alcoholics, I find a great many who have grown away from the Fellowship. Many say they no longer find interest in meetings. About those who have attained some degree of emotional maturity and spiritual growth and are happy, one should not complain, I suppose. But what a terrible loss their absence is for the newcomer, the beginner in AA! How much these successful people could contribute to the beginner who is so discouraged and depressed, so resentful of his enforced abstinence, so dependent upon others, or so ashamed, all too often, of his inadequacy and imagined weakness! One of the greatest incentives for continuing abstinence is the presence at meetings of those who have achieved sobriety and are happy. This is denied the unfortunate initiate if the older, successful members lose interest, in coming to meetings.

For those members, a newer and more stimulating activity might be found, to benefit the less fortunate ones. Visiting teams might be formed, made up of people who have attained, not just sobriety, but also insight, knowledge of human motivations, and a greater understanding of the many other factors involved in the problem of alcoholism. This work would involve them in a broader program than just maintaining their own sobriety. The public-health approach — emphasizing emotional, physiological, and psychological aspects of alcoholism — might supply the added incentive to learn even more about the problem which they have resolved for themselves, but which plagues so many others.

They might be stimulated to do more as citizens in correcting the problem in a general way, rather than working only with individuals who have sought out AA. The ignorance of alcoholism that still prevails is difficult to understand, but it exists, and knowledgeable members of AA can do much to dispel it.

For the alcohol-dependent, escape into unreality is what he seeks. This is the so-called comfort one gets from alcohol — make-believe, unreality. Once the alcoholic understands the desirability of accepting reality, to the best of his ability and within the limits which we all have, he has taken a step toward maturity. The difference between the mentally healthy person and the unhealthy one is the ability to face the realities of life. Some can take more than others. To aspire to heights of accomplishment greater than one has a capacity for achieving means continual frustration. And when the individual cannot take these frustrations and will not accept the fact that he has limitations, he is prone to blame others and to avoid self-honesty by escape through alcohol addiction. Normal escapes — such as reading, movies, television, sports, hobbies — are abandoned once alcohol takes over.

Many old concepts in regard to alcohol and alcoholism must be revised. The idea that the individual suffering from alcoholism must be ready for treatment is no longer valid. He must be induced to accept treatment long before he is ready to ask for it. This necessitates a tremendous educational program for the entire population, alerting them to the dangers of alcohol and to the very earliest signs of dependence upon the drug, whether psychological or physiological. Since, in most cases, the psychological effects precede the physiological, these signs must be readily recognized. It is to this end that we must devote time and effort, so that the interest of the medical profession and AA together will be to help the recovery of the sufferers. To bring to the attention of those in the early stages the necessity for treatment is the end to which we must all devote our efforts.

Marvin A. Block, MD
February 1974

༄

Our Mutual Sins

There are seven deadly sins—or errors, if you prefer that word—which keep our two worlds apart. I mean the world of the non-alcoholic professionals engaged in treating alcoholics, and the world of alcoholics sober in AA who are engaged in carrying the message of sobriety to still active alcoholics.

The first deadly sin (excuse me, error) is that of ignorance. Many persons who should be in a position to know the rudiments of alcoholism just don't. They are ignorant—not ignorant persons, but ignorant about the problem. Here is a case where a bartender may be more learned than a doctor or a judge.

It is a sad fact that the diagnosis of alcoholism escapes many a physician. Even when he is confronted with all the signs and symptoms of alcoholism, the unknowing physician, along with many others, may offer the statement: "You're no more an alcoholic than I am" or "Why don't you taper off with a little beer?"

Ignorance, then, is perhaps our first and gravest error. It allows some of us to offer medications, and sometimes wrong quantities of them, that only abet or worsen the alcoholic's problem.

But ignorance exists on the part of many others. It confounds the alcoholic's spouse for a long while, often until she finds her way to Al-Anon. It confuses the early alcoholic who, sensing that something is wrong with him, wanders about hopelessly like a tuberculosis victim of the Middle Ages who, spitting blood, did not know what was wrong or what to do.

The second error is that of fear. Fear about alcoholism confounds all of us, those who should be in a position to help, as well as the alcoholic himself.

The physician often acts out of fear of offending both the alcoholic and his spouse, as though alcoholism were a dirty word. The doctor nesitates to name it and talk about it. The employer fires the alcoholic for other reasons without attempting to talk openly about the real problem. The wife hides it from herself, family and friends. All out of fear.

The alcoholic must come to face his alcoholism; it need not be feared if it can be understood. The ability to speak without fear, to speak with understanding and directness, is most necessary in order to cut through the facade of the man still drinking. You who do Twelfth Step work know this very well.

The third error is that of omnipotence which is practiced a great deal by all of us, both alcoholic and nonalcoholic. The superior attitude which says, "I've got all the answers and I am holier than thou" affects many a Twelfth Step worker as well as many a physician, spouse, court or well-meaning friend. It consists of such advice as: "You must use willpower." "You mustn't be weak." "Snap out of it." "You gotta have guts." The omnipotent twelfth-stepper says, "Do it my way."

We doctors practice omnipotence when we believe that a magic medicine or rigid forms of psychotherapy alone will do the trick. When our omnipotence fails to bring about the desired results, we become angry and say the alcoholic won't cooperate. The omnipotent doctor ends up talking only to himself.

As for omnipotence on the part of the alcoholic, I need not dwell on that. It deludes the alcoholic while drinking and it sneaks up on him when abstinent. For this he needs the continued reminder and support of AA.

The fourth error is that of resentment, anger. It is committed on both sides of the fence. Usually, after omnipotence falls flat on its face, the physician is apt to become disillusioned, then resentful and angry. This feeling may easily spread to his attitude about all alcoholics. Since he doesn't understand them and they have not responded to his omnipotent methods he concludes that they are not worth helping or that they cannot be helped. His resentment may be openly expressed.

The spouse, the employer, the law itself, having gone through all the steps of ignorance, fear and omnipotence, may take on an attitude of open anger and resentment. The bitter-end point is reached when divorce occurs not only between the alcoholic and his spouse but between the alcoholic and his entire world.

I need not mention the extent to which resentment and anger bog down the alcoholic's life. Along with omnipotence it is perhaps the chief problem with which he has to contend.

The fifth error is that of dishonesty. The doctor commits this error whenever he sidesteps the issue of alcoholism and calls it something else. Hospitals practice it insofar as they may admit alcoholics under some diagnosis other than alcoholism. One of my medical friends who does treat alcoholics and treats them quite successfully, regularly admits his alcoholics under the diagnosis of singultus, i.e., hiccough. It is the only way he can get them a bed in certain hospitals.

The alcoholic who has not accomplished true sobriety practices this form of dishonesty also. So long as he cons himself into giving only lip service to the principles of AA he deludes himself.

The sixth error I call idolatry. It may exist in those who are in a position to help the alcoholic as well as the alcoholic himself. Idolatry is nothing more than losing touch with a power greater than ourselves. By whatever name we may want to designate this power, either as God, nature, the forces of the universe, love or as a philosophy of life, no one can hope to help the alcoholic who does not feel the existence of this power, and no alcoholic is safe without it. The worship of no pill, no machine, no special technique of intellectualized psychology will do us any good in the absence of this belief. In what I call idolatry we take to worshiping something other than a Higher Power. We take to worshiping a special system of treatment or, in the case of the alcoholic, worshiping the bottle.

In idolatry, both physician and alcoholic are left in a chasm of defeat.

The seventh and final error is that of indolence. It is committed by society as a whole. In our indolence we fail to do more than we are already doing about alcoholism. We are not doing enough to dispel ignorance. We are not doing enough to dispel fear.

We are not doing enough to bend to our purposes all that we now know to be effective: the proper handling of early alcoholics, whether it be at home, in the doctor's office, on the job, in jail, in our hospitals and institutions. More teaching about alcoholism in medical schools and to the public at large. Provision of more and better facilities in hospitals. More sobering-up stations, outpatient clinics and community-sponsored halfway houses. In all these areas we commit the error of indolence.

There can no longer be the world of the nonalcoholic and, opposed to it, the world of the alcoholic. We need one world if we are to be effective together in helping alcoholics.

I think now that I have given my list of our mutual sins, it would be to the point to go back a bit and review my own experience.

Five years ago I attended my first AA convention. I was quite new to alcoholism at that time. I then believed that the alcoholic could change if you just listened to his unconscious long enough and could understand him properly. I felt that personal interest, understanding and psychiatric interpretations were sufficient. I didn't understand the alcoholic's unstoppability, the fact that he already understood his unconscious better than I could ever know it, the need for a crisis in his life, and the constant reminder necessary to keep his ego down to human size. I certainly didn't understand AA.

At that AA convention I found myself very much alone. I was a stranger who could not understand the language being spoken. Even the few doctors I met at the convention, good AA members, didn't seem to speak my language, or perhaps I didn't speak theirs. To add hurt to my loneliness I heard AA speaker after speaker get up on the podium and rib the hell out of the doctors who had tried to treat them. I remember one young lady who with a flip of her cigarette announced, "So I went to this doctor and he tried this, and I went to that doctor and he tried that, and then there was the psychiatrist who kept me five years on the couch. But I kept on drinking!"

I was uncomfortable and a little angry.

Only on the way home did I see that this was a good experience for me. The AA speakers had played their role as devil's advocates and by so doing had jarred me into taking another look, which was good for me.

I saw that instead of one world, vitally concerned and working cooperatively on the problem of alcoholism, we have two worlds: the world of the (sober) alcoholic and the world of the nonalcoholic. A high brick wall sometimes seems to separate us, and I am not quite sure how it got there. There are errors on both sides of this wall, but let me now be a devil's advocate, in the pages of AA's magazine, and say how I see this operating in some AA members. I am speaking of those few but particular members of AA who sometimes give the impression of being so isolationist, so frightened about maintaining their sobriety, and still so angry with the rest of the world that I would call them the reactionaries of AA. (I know full well that these also exist on the other side of the wall, among nonalcoholics.)

There are probably many reasons why some few abstinent alcoholics feel the need to keep hostile fires going to maintain two worlds in alcoholism. Some have had experience in the hands of nonalcoholic helpers which they feel were harmful to them. Others, in the course of their Twelfth Step work are irked by the mismanagement of fledgling AAs by professional persons. I suspect many others cannot understand why anyone, not an alcoholic himself, could possibly be interested in the problem of alcoholism, want to help, and have something useful to offer. They perpetrate the myth that "you have to be an alcoholic to help an alcoholic." To these few extremes, to reactionaries, I would say, "Come out of it. As you come forward to accept and understand and help educate the nonalcoholic world, you will help erase the boundaries that divide our two worlds."

The respect which AA holds in the nonalcoholic world need not be emphasized here. This respect is immense. You need not and should not feel sensitive or apologetic any more than you need feel angry about the nonalcoholic's difficulty in understanding alcoholism. I suspect that most nonalcoholics are not as much "against" the alcoholic as puzzled and troubled by him. I suggest that AAs help these nonalcoholics to get unpuzzled and untroubled.

There are those who feel that AA is the one and only method of attaining abstinence and sobriety. It is similar to believing there is only one true church for alcoholics. This is not entirely true. Many different kinds of people become alcoholics and there are many different possible answers. Each person must find the answer which fits him, in his own way.

But lest these remarks be disastrously misconstrued, let me add that "other ways" are not in competition with AA, that AA is far and ahead, in my opinion, the most readily workable way that I know of. And I must certainly add that AA has never hurt anyone (although there are a few practicing alcoholics who would like to blame their drinking on AA which they "once tried"). Most important of all, I hope no one now safely in AA slips into the fallacy that he can "go it alone" or that he now dare try some other ephemeral way of achieving sobriety without AA.

Harry K. Elkins, MD
April 1966

∾

Message Carrier Extraordinary

For almost as many years as I've been sober (eight), it has been my privilege to address nonalcoholic groups of every variety on the subject of AA. Several years ago, I became a member of the Public Information Committee of New York Intergroup. These engagements have since increased to a degree that, I can hope, reflects expanding awareness of our unique solution to the problem of alcoholism.

Originally, speaking in high school and college classes, I was stunned at the response. I assumed that the relative inexperience and lack of prejudice in so youthful an audience were responsible for their consistent warmth and enthusiasm. I told them of my own feelings of alienation and discomfort as a teenager, my rebellious conduct, my search for workable values, and my descent into acute alcoholism, triggered by that first drink, while still in high school. They were attentive as I described my doomed attempts to overcome my tensions in college and my all-out, futile efforts to abstain from starting the chain reaction of abnormal drinking all over again.

They seemed to understand that the alcoholic is physiologically sensitive to depressant drugs—that beer and whiskey, not pot and pills, were the things to dare in the 1940s — that some of them present were already, or would prove to be, addiction-prone.

Usually, I remembered to observe that when I crept into AA, after nearly twenty years of battling alcoholism with ever-decreasing success, I was released from my fatal obsession, but was still emotionally pre-adolescent. They reacted affirmatively when I remarked that one can't meet the crises in life by depending on a drug (no matter what the drug) instead of on one's own heart and mind and soul and on God — and still expect to mature. The extreme awareness of today's youth is known to all of us. What surprised me was the depth and range of it.

There was always time for a brief description of the Fellowship and its history, the practice of living each day, the types of meetings, and the sponsor system, and a short explanation of each of the Twelve Steps as they apply to the mental, physical, and spiritual aspects of alcoholism. No one ever snickered when I spoke of finding my own faith in God through the gradual change in attitude engendered by these Steps.

All this took about twenty minutes, more or less, depending on the allotted time. The most important part of the engagement, to me, was the question-and-answer free-for-all that followed. Once, when I spoke before close to 600 high-school students and the graduating class, a boy at the rear of the hall quavered, "Aren't you ever going to get married?" That brought down the house. On another occasion, I addressed a larger student body, filled with children from impoverished areas where there was a considerable pill and drug problem. As I left the stage of the auditorium, the students rose en masse, cheering and applauding until I was out of sight — and far from dry of eye. Those cheers were for AA, not for me, and I felt gratitude and love for our Fellowship.

Since those early experiences, I, too, have been graduated, in a sense. Last year found me confronted on various occasions by student nurses, medical students, psychiatrists, adult psychology students, and the inevitable, heartening array of overweight ladies with their similar, humiliating compulsion. Nothing in life could have thrilled me more than being asked to address a church congregation at their regular Sunday service.

Everywhere, the reception has seemed the same. AA is respected among the most diverse age groups. No one appears prepared to argue with success. I feel support, publicly and privately, for what we are all trying to do — in our own individual ways and places, with God's help.

That's how a gal who used to hang over the bar at the smartest joint in town, looking for her next martini (on a good day), gets her kicks these days. And I thought I couldn't survive without drinking!

M. L. A.

Queens, New York

March 1970

꒰

Getting Help

I used to lie to doctors on a regular basis. Lots of alcoholics do that — maybe all of us do. But as an active alcoholic, I spent a lot of years wanting to stop drinking. So I would take my symptoms to doctors — physicians, psychiatrists, even dentists — hoping against hope that they would say "Your symptoms come from your drinking. You must stop drinking." And with that medical command, I believed, I would be able to stop.

The thing is that even with that goal in mind, whenever one of these professionals would ask about my alcohol consumption, I would lie. This disease will do anything to protect itself.

When I first started coming to meetings, I heard the suggestion that newcomers get a thorough physical checkup. I also heard people talking about having let their teeth and their bodies fall apart during their drinking. Luckily, I told myself, I was in good health: I hadn't let myself get that bad — and anyway, didn't I repeatedly seek medical attention while drinking? The truth was, of course, that I was afraid, still, to admit my alcoholism.

As it happened, I had not been sober very long when I had occasion to go to a clinic where I was asked to fill out a medical history form including questions about my drinking and drug habits. What a relief to write "I am a recovering alcoholic." What freedom to be able to tell the truth!

Since then, for better or worse, I've had many opportunities to tell that truth to professional helpers — physicians, dentists, psychiatrists, lawyers, accountants, even judges. AA works hard, through its CPC (Cooperation with the Professional Community) projects, to make these helpers aware of alcoholism as a disease, of AA's program, and of the sometimes special needs of alcoholics. My own experiences in dealing with these very essential nonalcoholics bear witness to the importance of these CPC efforts. I realize that my personal encounters with members of the professional community have a variety of positive results: Not only does my truth telling benefit me, it also helps the professionals and through them, perhaps, another suffering alcoholic.

For instance, when I needed to find a physician in a new community, I asked around my meetings and learned that a local alcoholism organization kept a list of doctors who treated alcoholics. From that list, I picked the one nearest to me — and quickly found that, as newly sober as I was, I knew more about alcoholism than he did. But he did understand the seriousness of my purpose in staying sober and staying away from risky medications. As our relationship has developed, I have helped him learn a lot more about this disease. I've given him CPC pamphlets, helped him to understand why his alcoholic patients can't simply stop drinking when he tells them they should, described the difference between being "on the wagon" and being sober, and explained why meetings continue to be essential after more than five years of sobriety. He has never failed to be supportive of my recovery. When I was hospitalized, he took up my cause with an even more naive specialist, and he once told me during a checkup, "You look 200 percent better than when I first saw you. Whatever you're doing, it must work."

After I'd been sober a while, I decided, with my sponsor's support, to start psychotherapy again. I had been in therapy while I was drinking, and it had helped resolve many of my life problems, but not my drinking. My former therapist believed that by resolving my underlying conflicts, the drinking could be relieved — the alcoholic's dream. This time, of course, I needed a different approach, so I gathered names from people I respected and went therapist shopping. I told each prospect that I was a recovering alcoholic; that my primary purpose was staying sober; but that I had some conflicts that required professional help. All of them professed to having experience in helping alcoholics, so I questioned them: "Tell me what you know about Step Six," for instance. The one who answered that got a second interview. As it turned out, though he was not an alcoholic himself, he called himself a "recovering psychiatrist." He believed that "the real healing is in the rooms; I am just an adjunct." When I compare that with tales I've heard in meetings of psychiatrists who not only don't support their patients' sobriety, but work against it, I feel especially glad that I put in the footwork finding mine. I gained a great deal from my sessions with him, partly because I was sober and telling the truth, of course, but also because I was dealing with a doctor who told me to not drink and go to meetings and, when confronted by a particularly knotty issue, suggested that I'd better pray about it.

One can't expect that kind of indepth support from every professional, of course. But these experiences helped make it easier for me to put my recovery up front in every medical situation and to better evaluate the difference between an emergency room doctor who says, "Three years sober? That's wonderful!" and one who sneers, "Well, the best treatment for your pain would be a tranquilizer, but of course you wouldn't take that!"

Telling strangers about my alcoholism is one thing; telling professionals who have treated me during my "lying years" is another. So I was nervous about revealing my previous drinking to the dentist I had used for years. I had been told, though, that this was important, because dentists sometimes use dubious drugs (including, sometimes, psychoactive "boosters" to novocaine) and because my chemically new body might react differently to pain and painkillers. So on my first sober visit to the dentist I swallowed hard and told him the truth. He didn't bat an eye — and immediately substituted plain water for the 40-proof mouthwash he'd had in the "please rinse" cup. I've learned that I seem to need more novocaine than I used to, and sometimes I'm afraid to ask — so he pays attention to how I'm reacting.

In short, when I've put my sobriety first and been honest with doctors, I've not only protected myself, but I've gotten the special help I've needed.

The same has been true with using other professionals whose skills have been required because of the gifts of sober living. I was able to find a lawyer in my home group, but only after I'd heard him share often enough to feel that he was trustworthy. I've learned firsthand, though, that being sober doesn't guarantee competence in a professional: A recovering accountant to whom I was referred proved to be a near disaster, so I went back to my pre-AA accountant and fessed up. This was important, not only because of the increased, and increasingly complex, prosperity that has come with sobriety but also because a confrontation with the IRS can be a sobriety-threatening experience! When my accountant had successfully handled an IRS audit for me, she said, "You deserve a great big drink. No, a great big piece of chocolate cake!" The message gets spread in unexpected directions.

It seems that some judges have gotten the message, too. In all my years of drinking, I never had to appear before a judge. Sobriety means showing up, though, including showing up for jury duty, which frightened me. My sponsor told me that if I was uncomfortable about any aspect of it, including the possibility of being sequestered and cut off from my support network, I could speak up. Still, I was surprised when, after describing in detail the case at hand, which involved drugs and drinking, the judge invited anyone who felt uneasy — "such as members of AA" — to approach the bench. As I walked up, I mentally prepared a lengthy explanation, which proved to be unnecessary. The judge said, "You're excused, and you'll find plenty of cases that don't involve drugs. Thank you for being honest with us."

Being honest — is that all it takes? Like everything else I've learned in the rooms of AA, getting help from professionals — something that used to terrify me into silence and paralysis — is, indeed, almost that simple.

I begin by being honest about my need for help. Then I ask for suggestions in getting that help, and I honestly try to follow them. Keeping my sobriety first, I am honest with the professionals I use and, having turned over an important aspect of my life to them, I must be honest in my efforts to follow their advice. I also check with my sponsor when I'm uncertain. Then, when the bills come in, AA keeps me honest again, so I do my best to pay them promptly. Having been open about my AA membership, I wouldn't want to give AAs a bad credit reference!

All of this practice with professionals served me well when I was faced with sudden hospitalization. Though my sponsor, sponsees, and AA friends were available as much as possible, I was essentially on my own. I told every hospital interviewer I encountered, from the admitting room through specialists and floor nurses, that I was a recovering alcoholic. I explained that this fact had potential medical implications, and insisted on being consulted prior to any medication. Still, lying in a hospital bed for the first time in my adult life, I was feeling frightened and alone when I had the unexpected thought, "What this is about is showing how a sober person does it." I wasn't sure what that meant until I was almost ready to go home. I had been unable to attend any of the hospital's AA meetings, but an alcoholism counselor on the staff came to visit, with my chart in her hand. To my surprise she said, "You've done some important twelfth-step work here."

What did she mean? "These nurses and interns and aides are very accustomed to seeing active alcoholics. But no matter how much educating I try to do, they have a hard time associating 'alcoholic' with 'sober alcoholic.' They find it hard to believe that you're an alcoholic — but you've shown them by your attitude, by the network of support you have, that AA works. Thank you!"

Thank you — for helping me to learn to be honest even with outside professionals. And for being able to say those simple-but-not-easy words, "I am a recovering alcoholic."

Those few words not only help to protect my sobriety by keeping me out of medical and emotional crises that could trigger my disease, but when doctors, judges, lawyers, and others have evidence that AA works — that there's hope — they'll pass that on.

Sara G.

New York, New York

December 1989

༢

Let It Begin With Me

My name is Jim Estelle and I'm a grateful nonalcoholic. The fact that you all have let me share your joy in sobriety for some twenty or twenty-five years has allowed me to survive in what has become increasingly hazardous work. It got so hazardous last January that I decided to retire from it. I have thirty-two years of experience in corrections and very little expertise. If there were any experts in the business of corrections, I'd have had to go to work for a living about twenty-five years ago.

I want to encourage you all to tell your stories in a very special place to some very special people who can't come to you to hear those stories. I have some very strong and deep feelings about these people. Lurking in the background of the illness of alcoholism, which you all have found a way to control, are a lot of other tragic and traumatic results. One of the principal results is the incidence of crime that has alcoholism as its base. Some of you are familiar with that side effect, either directly or indirectly. And every one of us is involved indirectly with the side effect of crime, if for no other reason than the amount of money it costs us as citizens and taxpayers. If we could find a way to give away to the convicted felons in the United States what you in AA have found, we would have about 350,000 productive citizens more than we have today.

Crime is a lot like the weather. We all like to talk about it, but nobody knows what to do about it. You all do know what to do about it, though. I said there's no expertise in the field of corrections — well, there are two areas of expertise that we have not yet tapped. One is a Higher Power, and the second is the Fellowship of Alcoholics Anonymous. We in the discipline of corrections have not had the good sense to tap those two resources — those two potentials for good — any more than we have. And you let us get away with it. That's your contribution to the rising incidence of crime, by the way. You all have heard and used the phrase "I am responsible"? Well, we are collectively and individually responsible for our failure to give away the treasure of the Fellowship — sobriety. Compounding that felony, we have not insisted that we each have enough discipline to carry the message to one person who's ended up in trouble because of the illness of alcoholism. And you let me, as a professional correctional administrator, ignore the message.

You've all heard references to the court-ordered members of AA — "a pain in the butt." I hear that too many times. How often have all of us wished that we could get the message to somebody who needed it so much? We couldn't quite find the way. Well, some judge found a way, and he doesn't have the same constraints that we do. He's not bound by the Traditions. He's not bound by the Steps. But he knows this person needs help and he knows you've got it, and if you won't come to his sick alcoholic, he is sure going to keep sending his sick alcoholics to you.

I think it's high time those of us in and close to AA quit complaining about the people who are coming for the message of sobriety, no matter what their motivation or lack of it is, and start sharing what we've got to share with those folks. We can stop a lot of these still-suffering alcoholics right then and there if we'll just begin to share the way you have shared with your friends and neighbors and the alcoholics whom you've twelfth-stepped. But we need to share with all of them, no matter how they come to the groups — share with them the same way someone shared with you. Some of them are going to have to go to jail, but we have the potential of reducing the number significantly.

If you wonder where all the twelfth-stepping has gone, you don't have to look farther than your friendly corner jail. Suffering alcoholics are gathered there like quail under a piece of brush in the rain — waiting for you. You don't have to go look for them. You don't have to wait for that lonely call at three in the morning. Your jails are full of them, and they're waiting for someone just like you; and all they want is what you've found—sobriety. You may not know it yet, but some of you have some pretty subtle ways of motivating and encouraging and enlightening those people.

Then there are a few of them who aren't going to get the message, and you and I both know it — they're on their way to prison in spite of all we might do for them, or to them, or with them. Well, that seems to be what it takes for some of us to learn. I had to spend thirty-two years of my life "in prisons," so to speak, before I learned I was working on the wrong end of the problem — after the fact. AA members can work on it before the fact. They're in prison and they're going to be back with you — they're going to be back in the community. You've got to bridge the gap with them. You need to work with them when they're on parole, but there's so much that can be done in view of the emphasis that's being placed on DWIs in today's world and with the numbers of them going to detox centers and with the numbers of them still going to drunk tanks and spending thirty and sixty and ninety days in jail. There are so many who could be stopped from going any further. What a spin-off. What several spin-offs we could get from our response.

How do we do it? Well, your General Service Conference approved a workbook for correctional committees. Some of you have more experience and more insight into the Fellowship and its relation to crime and its relation to institutions than the Workbook has. But there are a lot of our members out there who would like to get involved and have never been involved for whom this workbook will serve well. The Conference told us, "Get it on press and get it out to the folks who want it and need it."

It wouldn't hurt any of us to be seen in the company of a sheriff, or a jailer, or a warden — not in the shape you're all in today. It wouldn't hurt you a bit, and it would help their image — I guarantee you it would help their image immensely if they were seen in your company. We have something they need. They need something in their jail; they need something in their prison that works. They haven't got it today and I've been telling them that for the last ten years of my career. You have something that works! Twelfth-stepping with people in serious trouble adds a totally new dimension to your service in this Fellowship. Those of you who have experienced this know what I'm talking about. Those of you who haven't experienced this special kind of twelfth-stepping are denying yourselves one of the great satisfying service experiences available to us all.

I mentioned the phrase "I am responsible." There's one more phrase I like that goes hand in glove with responsibility: "Let it begin with me."

W. Jim Estelle, Jr.
July 1985

AA Pioneers

That AA ever got off the ground is a miracle in itself. Our beginnings were so tenuous, so seemingly random. And yet, there were many AA pioneers, both alcoholics and nonalcoholics, who believed it could work, who saw the incredible possibilities and gave tirelessly of themselves to shield, water, and provide light for the seeds out of which our Fellowship would grow.

With nothing more than a powerful faith and the novel idea of one alcoholic helping another, our AA pioneers reached out time and again, lovingly offering a way out to countless alcoholics who hitherto had known only suffering and pain. According to Bill W., as he expressed in the October 1947 Grapevine, "In actuality, AA has scores of 'founders,' men and women without whose special contributions AA might never have been." Together, they blazed a trail that millions have followed.

༄

Dr. Bob: The Man and the Physician

It is very difficult to speak of Dr. Bob without going into eulogistic superlatives. While he lived, he laughed them off. And now, though he is dead, I feel that he still laughs them off. I sat beside him many times at the speakers' table and watched him squirm as some florid introduction was being given him. Many a chairman of the meeting strove to rise to the responsibility of introducing him by referring to him as co-founder of the "greatest, most wonderful, most magnificent, most momentous movement of all time." Dr. Bob whispered to me on one of these occasions, "The speaker certainly takes in a lot of territory and plenty of time."

While Dr. Bob thoroughly appreciated the spirit of personal gratitude that usually prompted such superlatives, he never took them seriously as applicable to himself. He rose up to tell with all humility the simple story of an alcoholic's return to sobriety. He seldom called upon his vast experience with others. He simply repeated in different ways the story of one man's great return. And that was his own.

He could have gone scientific and statistical, for he heard more confessions of sprees and lost weekends than anyone else alive. But he never did it that way. He always remained plain. Dr. Bob had once been lost in an alcoholic fog himself. He recalled that he, too, had been proud, resentful, full of rancor, cocky, self-sufficient, and selfish. But whether he spoke at the banquet table or ministered to an alcoholic in the ward, he was kind but firm, serious and sympathetic, always unmindful of race, color, creed, or previous state of alcoholic servitude.

Dr. Bob was a humble man. His humility was born, no doubt, of his humiliations before his good wife, Anne, and his colleagues in the medical profession. This led to the great step of becoming humble before his God. Here was the crisis in his life: at last, he found the

God who he knew would help him if he would only place a humble confidence in him. This is the story of Dr. Bob. It is the story, too, of the Twelve Steps that logically follow, once the situation is faced with honest realism.

Looking back over his life, one might say Dr. Bob was two people, two personalities, even in his drinking days. After his return to sobriety, he still remained two personalities. As he made his rounds through St. Thomas Hospital, he did so as Dr. R. H. S., medical practitioner. But as he came to Room 390, the alcoholic ward, he put off the cloak of science and professionalism and became just plain Dr. Bob, a man eager, willing, and able to help his fellow man. As he left the hospital each day, two men went out through the door — one a great MD, the other a great man.

It was quite natural that Dr. S. sought hospitalization for alcoholics. He had been sending the sick to St. Thomas Hospital for years, and alcoholism to him was a sickness as real as pneumonia, but not so easy to treat. The new treatment was to be physical, psychological, social, and spiritual. The whole patient was to be treated, because the whole man was sick.

Many of his colleagues in the medical profession disagreed with Dr. S., some bitterly. It was fortunate that he had been associated with the nursing sisters at St. Thomas Hospital. It was very fortunate, even providential, that he met the Sisters of Charity of St. Augustine. For in the long, long history of their order, they had taken care of all manner of disease, dereliction, and misfortune, and they were now willing to try the newer method of treating alcoholism. Thus, for the first time, a ward in a general hospital was opened to Alcoholics Anonymous.

Dr. S. and the sisters soon learned to diagnose more accurately and prescribe more effectively. Here was a new type of patient needing a new type of treatment. The disorder seemed more on the psychological and spiritual than on the physical side. Here was a patient whose thinking was all beclouded; whose attitudes were wrong; whose philosophy of life was all mixed up; whose sense of values was distorted; whose spiritual life was nonexistent. The patient was indeed a definite challenge to the skill, patience, and prayer of all who worked at the hospital with Dr. S. in the noble art of healing a terribly wounded personality.

What success attended his efforts, as well as the efforts of the sisters and all who worked with the many patients who passed through that ward, is now a matter of history. It will ever remain a monument to the memory of R. H. S., MD — and Dr. Bob, the man.

J. G.
Ohio
September 1978

~

He Kept the Faith

Bill D., AA Number Three, died in Akron Friday night, September 17th, 1954. That is, people say he died, but he really didn't. His spirit and works are today alive in the hearts of uncounted AAs and who can doubt that Bill already dwells in one of those many Mansions in the Great Beyond.

Nineteen years ago last summer, Dr. Bob and I saw him for the first time. Bill lay on his hospital bed and looked at us in wonder.

Two days before this, Dr. Bob had said to me, "If you and I are going to stay sober, we had better get busy." Straightway Bob called Akron's City Hospital and asked for the nurse on the receiving ward. He explained that he and a man from New York had a cure for alcoholism. Did she have an alcoholic customer on whom it could be tried? Knowing Bob of old, she jokingly replied, "Well, Doctor, I suppose you've already tried it yourself?"

Yes, she did have a customer — a dandy. He just arrived in DTs.

Had blacked the eyes of two nurses, and now they had him strapped down tight. Would this one do? After prescribing medicines, Dr. Bob ordered, "Put him in a private room. We'll be down as soon as he clears up."

We found we had a tough customer in Bill. According to the nurse, he had been a well-known attorney in Akron and a City Councilman. But he had landed in the Akron City Hospital four times in the last six months. Following each release, he got drunk even before he could get home.

So here we were, talking to Bill, the first "man on the bed." We told him about our drinking. We hammered it into him that alcoholism was an obsession of the mind, coupled to an allergy of the body. The obsession, we explained, condemned the alcoholic to drink against his will and the allergy, if he went on drinking, could positively guarantee his insanity or death. How to unhook that fatal compulsion, how to restore the alcoholic to sanity, was, of course, the problem.

Hearing this bad news, Bill's swollen eyes opened wide. Then we took the hopeful tack, we told what we had done: how we got honest with ourselves as never before, how we had talked our problems out with each other in confidence, how we tried to make amends for harm done others, how we had then been miraculously released from the desire to drink as soon as we had humbly asked God, as we understood him, for guidance and protection.

Bill didn't seem too impressed. Looking sadder than ever, he wearily ventured, "Well, this is wonderful for you fellows, but can't be for me. My case is so terrible that I'm scared to go out of this hospital at all. You don't have to sell me religion, either. I was one time a deacon in the church and I still believe in God. But I guess He doesn't believe much in me."

Then Dr. Bob said, "Well, Bill, maybe you'll feel better tomorrow. Wouldn't you like to see us again?"

"Sure I would," replied Bill, "Maybe it won't do any good. But I'd like to see you both, anyhow. You certainly know what you are talking about."

Looking in next day, we found Bill with his wife, Henrietta. Eagerly he pointed to us saying, "These are the fellows I told you about, they are the ones who understand."

Bill then related how he had lain awake nearly all night. Down in the pit of his depression, new hope had somehow been born. The thought flashed through his mind, "If they can do it, I can do it." Over and over he said this to himself. Finally, out of his hope, there burst conviction. Now he was sure. Then came a great joy. At length peace stole over him and he slept.

Before our visit was over Bill suddenly turned to his wife and said, "Go fetch my clothes, dear. We're going to get up and get out of here." Bill D. walked out of that hospital a free man, never to drink again. AA's Number One Group dates from that very day.

The force of the great example that Bill set in our pioneering time will last as long as AA itself.

Bill kept the faith — what more could we say?

Bill W.
November 1954

Ebby

While attending the annual Bill W. dinner in New York in October 1963, I noticed a man with a sad expression seated at the table that Bill and Lois shared with close friends. Since the general atmosphere in the large banquet room was festive, his sadness seemed out of place. Someone told me he was Ebby T., the friend who had called on Bill in late 1934 to bring him the Oxford Group's spiritual message that helped Bill get sober and helped form AA.

Several months later, during one of the last discussions I ever had with Bill, he told me that he had been able to place Ebby in a country rest home in upstate New York. Ebby died two years later from emphysema, the same affliction that would claim Bill's life in 1971.

Ebby's physical problems had been compounded by his frequent bouts with alcohol during the years since he had carried the message to Bill. His was the kind of story that causes continuing anguish in AA: a wonderful burst of initial sobriety followed by a devastating slip and then a pattern of repeated binges despite his best efforts and those of his friends. He had a tortured life, and yet there were times when he struggled valiantly to put his demons to rest.

I never actually met Ebby, but I kept learning more about him as the years passed. While serving as a contributing writer to *Pass It On* in 1980 and 1981, I had access to the correspondence that flowed between him and Bill. There was also an opportunity to spend a day with Margaret, the kindly nurse who cared for Ebby during his last two years of life.

In Albany, New York's capital city, there is archival information in the state library about Ebby's distinguished family members and their achievements in politics and business. Three members of the T. family were Albany mayors, and one lost a gubernatorial nomination by a very narrow margin. Ebby's parents were also prominent in social and church affairs. An assistant to the mayor at that time told me "you couldn't find a better family than the T.s" and put me in touch with Ebby's nephew, Ken T., Jr. When I returned to Albany some years later, Ken took me to visit Ebby's grave in the Albany Rural Cemetery, just north of the city.

There's no denying that Ebby was the "lost sheep" of the family, but it never completely rejected him or lost hope that he might some-day recover. His last surviving brother, Ken T., Sr., stayed loyal to him right up to the time of his own death, just a few months before Ebby's passing.

But if Ebby had a friend who was unfailingly loyal and devoted, it was Bill W., who always called Ebby his sponsor and seemingly moved heaven and earth in trying to help Ebby regain sobriety. Indeed, it almost seemed that Bill threw his own good judgment out the window and became an "enabler" when Ebby was involved. The late Yev G., a member of the Manhattan Group since 1941, told me in 1980 that Bill seemed to lose all perspective when Ebby went off on another drunk. Yev recalled it this way:

"Bill was so definitely concerned about Ebby and so fond of him and felt so grateful and indebted to him that he would do anything rather than have anything happen to Ebby. Some of us were Bill's selected emissaries to find Ebby when he went out on one of his episodes. We knew his watering holes, the rooming houses, and the places where he went. So we'd get him and bring him back in the group, and he'd go along very well. But we had to observe, really, that Bill did not treat Ebby with the same kind of approach that he realistically would with the average kind of alcoholic member we had in those days in New York."

But even Bill became exasperated with Ebby at times, and this is revealed in some of his correspondence with and about Ebby. But he never lost hope that Ebby would recover, and years after his own recovery he would tell Ebby of his gratitude. It was an astonishing friendship, and one early AA told me that Bill and Ebby were almost like brothers.

A brief outline of Ebby's life goes this way: he was born in Albany in 1896, the youngest of five brothers. His father headed a family-owned foundry that manufactured railroad-car wheels, and Ebby entered life with the proverbial silver spoon in his mouth. Like his brothers, he attended Albany Academy, a prestigious private school that is highly regarded and whose graduates usually go on to college. But though his brothers excelled at the academy, Ebby was a lackluster student and did not graduate.

The family spent their summers in the resort town of Manchester, Vermont, seven miles south of Bill's hometown, East Dorset. Ebby's

father was a golfing partner of Robert Todd Lincoln, a wealthy indus-
trialist and the only son of Abraham Lincoln to reach adulthood.
Lois's family was also a member of this social group, the "summer
people" who awed Bill as he was growing up. Although Bill felt
inferior in status to Ebby's family and Lois's family, he was something
of a hero to other boys in Manchester because of his skill as a baseball
pitcher. Ebby remembered meeting him in 1910 or '11 and perhaps
watched him play.

Ebby may have sipped a little wine on family occasions, but he
didn't have his real first drink until 1915, at age nineteen, when he
walked into Albany's Hotel Ten Eyck and ordered a glass of beer.
At about the same time, he went to work in the family business. By
the time the firm closed in 1922, Ebby was getting drunk frequently.
Later on in the nineteen-twenties he worked in the Albany office of a
brokerage firm, but there's reason to believe he was never a real pro-
ducer. In the meantime, Bill W. had become a New York stockbroker
and was soaring with the surging market on Wall Street.

In January 1929, Bill stopped in Albany on his way to visit friends
in Vermont, and he gave Ebby a call. He and Ebby spent the evening
drinking and then agreed on a daring way to arrive in Manchester:
by air, a risky action in those early days of aviation. They hired a
barnstorming pilot to fly them to Manchester, which had just built an
airfield, and they arrived, very drunk, the next day. Bill recalled
(as quoted in *Pass It On*): "We somehow slid out of the cockpit, fell on
the ground, and there we lay, immobile. Such was the history-making
episode of the first airplane ever to light at Manchester, Vermont."
Their drunken venture may have created an odd bond between Ebby
and Bill that would be among the reasons Ebby would call on him in
1934.

Ebby's drinking worsened, and by late 1932 he had become such an
embarrassment to his family that he slunk off to Manchester, and
moved back into his family's summer home. He had periods of sobriety, but by mid-1934 his drinking had led to troubles and arrests in

Manchester. While his brothers were still actively employed or in business, the family money supporting Ebby had largely run out. According to some tales circulated later, he sold some of the family furniture to buy booze.

About this time, several Oxford Group members in the area chose Ebby as a likely prospect for their spiritual message. They were Rowland H., Shep C., and Cebra G. He resisted their approach, but became more receptive when another drunken incident brought him before a judge in Bennington. He expected to be jailed for the weekend, but was permitted to go home on the promise that he would return — sober — on Monday.

And it was at this point, I think, that Ebby won a battle that became important for all of us. Waiting for him in the cellar at home were several bottles of his favorite ale, which he planned to drink immediately after the local constable let him off at the house. He was in agony when he raced down the stairs to get them. But then his promise to the judge stopped him cold, and he began to wrestle with his conscience. After a fierce struggle he took the bottles over to a neighbor. The action gave him peace. That was his last attempt to drink for two years and seven months.

I like to think of this moment as Ebby's Magnificent Victory. I've wondered whether, if he'd lost this struggle, he might not have stayed sober and been able to carry the message to Bill. In any case, he returned to court sober and was released to the custody of Rowland H., who then became what we AAs would call a sponsor. Along with giving Ebby a grounding in Oxford Group principles, Rowland took him to New York City. After staying with Shep for a short time, Ebby moved to Calvary Mission, run by Dr. Sam Shoemaker's Calvary Church on Gramercy Park.

One November night in 1934, Ebby came to see Bill, who was then living in Brooklyn with his wife, Lois. Ebby told Bill, "I've got religion," and while Bill drank gin and pineapple juice, Ebby recounted his friendship with Rowland, described the principles of the Oxford

Group (like the importance of absolute honesty when dealing with defects), and talked about his growing belief in God and the efficacy of prayer. Ebby's words, and his sober demeanor, stayed with Bill, who later recalled, "The good of what he said stuck so well that in no waking moment thereafter could I get that man and his message out of my head." Bill kept drinking, but he decided to pay a visit to the mission, which he did after stopping at a number of bars on the way and hooking up with a drunk Finnish fisherman. When he arrived at the mission, he ended up giving a kind of drunken monologue at the evening meeting where the derelict men gave testimonials about not drinking. On December 11, Bill checked himself back into Towns Hospital, where he'd previously been treated. Ebby visited him there, and a few days later, Bill had his "white light" experience and never took another drink.

Ebby stayed on in New York, continued to work with Bill, and moved in with Bill and Lois after Calvary Mission closed in 1936. But by 1937 he was back in Albany, working in a Ford factory. While he still worked with alcoholics and apparently kept up his Oxford Group connections, tensions were building up in his personal life. Finally, on a trip to New York City, he drank again, after two years and seven months of sobriety.

His life then became a nightmarish succession of binges followed by short periods of sobriety. He held jobs briefly and sometimes performed well for short periods of time. During World War II, for example, he worked as a Navy civilian employee and was well-liked by his superiors. He was given opportunities by other AA members, and both Bill W. and his older brother Jack sought ways to help him back to continuous sobriety and well-being. In the following years, he often lived with Bill and Lois for months at a time — something Lois tolerated for Bill's sake.

It also became a sort of a game by AA members to become the person who helped Ebby recover. In 1953, a New York member named Charlie M. collaborated with AA members in Dallas, Texas, to take

Ebby to the Lone Star state for treatment at a clinic run by Searcy W., an early member who still recalls his years with Ebby. After initial troubles, Ebby found sobriety in Texas and stayed there for eight years. He also found steady employment for several years.

It's clear that Ebby's Texas interlude was the best period of his adult life. He was lionized by grateful Texas people who went out of their way to meet him or hear him speak. In 1954, Ralph J. and his wife Mary Lee even invited Ebby for a two-month stay at their sheep ranch near Ozona, Texas, and loved every minute of his visit. Two members, Olie L. and Icky S., virtually adopted him, and Searcy became Ebby's Texas sponsor.

But one of Ebby's obsessions had been the belief that "finding the right woman" would be his salvation. He did find a woman in Texas who seemed to be the love of his life, but when she died suddenly, he began taking mood-changing pills and soon was drinking again. He returned to the New York area in late 1961 and stayed for a time with his brother Ken.

Bill W. had continued to help Ebby with occasional checks, and now he came forward again to manage Ebby's life more closely, partly because of Ebby's declining physical condition. With help from others, Bill had created a fund for Ebby to cover his expenses at a treatment-type facility. Health problems were closing in on Ebby, however, and it was clear that he could no longer live independently. And that's probably why Ebby appeared so sad when I saw him at Bill's banquet in 1963. He was in very poor health, to say nothing of the other demons that plagued him.

But there was a miracle of sorts waiting for Ebby. In the final two years of his life, he would find peace, sobriety, and tender loving care given by Margaret M. and her husband Mickey at their rest farm in Galway, near Saratoga Springs, New York. Symbolically enough, the farm was on a road named Peaceable Street!

Bill had met the M.s and when he learned that Margaret was in New York attending a nurse's convention, he asked her to come over to talk with him at GSO. She agreed to give Ebby care at the farm for seventy-five dollars a week — a cost Bill could easily manage with the fund and Ebby's Social Security payments.

Bill drove Ebby up to the rest farm in May 1964, and turned him over to Margaret and Mickey. Ebby was angry and defensive at first, but soon responded to their attempts to help him. Usually a likable person, Ebby even became popular with the other residents and awed them by his ability to work *The New York Times* crossword puzzles. The farm was only twenty-five miles from Albany, so he also had visits from his brother Ken and other friends and relatives. There couldn't have been a better place for Ebby's last years. Bill, writing to Ebby's old friends in Texas, would comment on the fine care Margaret was giving Ebby, and would also note that she had a good doctor on call.

When Ebby's brother Ken died in January 1966, Ebby was too weak to travel the twenty-five miles to Albany for the funeral. He seemed to lose the will to live after that, and one morning in March the housekeeper told Margaret that Ebby couldn't come down for breakfast. He was rushed to the nearby Ballston Spa hospital, where he died early in the morning on March 21.

Bill and Lois were on a trip to Mexico, but returned quickly for the funeral in Albany. It was a small funeral, and one woman who attended thought it symbolic that twelve persons were there to see him off. A brief notice in the local newspaper mentioned that Ebby was the brother of a former prominent mayor.

In death, Ebby rejoined his prominent family at the Albany Rural Cemetery, where he lies next to his brother Ken. The large plot is defined by the monument of his grandfather, who launched the family business and also served as Albany's mayor during the Civil War. (Ken, Jr., who was so generous in supplying information about Ebby and the family, passed away two months after showing me Ebby's grave. He is also buried nearby.)

I felt some of that gratitude myself when I visited the old farmhouse with Margaret in 1980. She had operated it after Mickey's death but finally closed it in 1979.

When AA members learn that I've become a student of Ebby's life, their first question is usually, "Did he die sober?" I believe, as did Ebby's Texas sponsor, Searcy W., that Ebby was sober two-and-a-half years when he died. This may have taken lots of supervision by Bill and Margaret, but he did put this much together in his final years. We should give him credit for that, because he gave us so much — particularly when he won the battle with ale that weekend in 1934. Without that magnificent victory, the outcome could have been much different for all of us.

Mel B.
Toledo, Ohio
September 1999

༣

Sister Mary Ignatia

Among the first friends of AA, few are so beloved as Sister Mary Ignatia, subject of this moving tribute from an AA who was helped by her years ago. November is Gratitude Month in AA: here is an occasion to remember that the vital strands of spiritual influence, information and help that went into the making of our Fellowship were woven almost entirely by nonalcoholics. Those were the old days, nearly thirty years past. Our earliest friends, young then, are older now; many of them have gone from us. Sister Mary Ignatia this year celebrated her Golden Anniversary as a nun; over twenty-five years of this life of service to God have been dedicated to the care and recovery of alcoholics and to the carrying of the AA message to uncounted thousands at St. Thomas Hospital, Akron, Ohio.

—The Editors

A startlingly large number of AAs, if asked to name the person who had been the greatest help to them in achieving sobriety, would name a nonalcoholic, Sister Mary Ignatia of the Roman Catholic order of the Sisters of Charity of St. Augustine.

How, we ask, could she, who had no experience of alcoholism itself, have had the compassion and complete understanding which she has shown for every tiny facet of the complex mess which the suffering alcoholic always is? The great spirit in her tiny earthly body has lived tirelessly, weaving golden threads of spiritual inspiration from one alcoholic to another, day after day, and year after year, whether her patient happened to be Protestant, Catholic, Jewish or of no religion at all.

Many have literally had body and soul, and early sobriety, held together by the never-ending strands of her love, concern, and dedication to the salvation of people like us. God moves in mysterious ways for all of us, but none of the wondrous mysteries of His grace could compare with the miracle of this tiny nun and her gift to our Fellowship.

Once as she stood contemplating a new alcoholic patient in miserable condition, a representative of the hospital, concerned with earthly practicalities, inquired whether adequate financial provision for the new patient had been made. The response, delivered with asperity, was, "I am interested in souls, not dollars."

On another occasion, she stood looking reflectively out the window and said mostly to herself, "That was a big step I took from music [her early interest] to alcohol." Indeed it was. Yet the greatest symphony of the finest master composer, in its most superb rendition, must seem small by comparison with the miracles in which her great spirit has played a vital part. Imagine a great stage on which might be assembled at one time, the thousands of recovered alcoholics whom she has helped. Then imagine a great auditorium in front of such a stage in which might be gathered the families, relatives, friends and other associates of those on the stage. That spectacle, were it possible, would surpass in beauty the greatest musical production of all time.

Our Lord told his disciples to go forth to preach the gospel and heal the sick. No servant of His has contributed more to the healing of alcoholism than she. Yet in her complete humility, we can hear her saying as one of the ancient physicians did, "All I do is bind the wounds. God is the Great Physician."

How does one express in words the gratitude and love so many of us feel towards Sister Mary Ignatia? The answer must be that it isn't possible. Only through what we are and what we do can the reality of this gratitude and love be demonstrated to her.

"Now is eternity; this very moment is eternity." That has been said by her to many of us, over and over again. For those of us who have learned to live one day at a time, often one minute at a time, perhaps this statement has a profound meaning which may not be shared by others. "Each moment of life is a gift from God, which when we are through with it, is deposited exactly as we left it, forever in eternity." Thanks to her, many of us have tried to improve the quality of deposits in God's eternity, knowing full well that our maximum will be a pitifully small contribution.

Words, even by a master in their use, if we had one, could not express the gratitude and love we have for this great healer of our common disease. Rather, we shall, we must, try to show it through action, in our own lives and in efforts to help others.

Anonymous
November 1964

✌

The Little Doctor Who Loved Drunks

Dr. William Duncan Silkworth 1873 - 1951

A drunk is lying on a bed in a hospital, and a doctor is sitting beside the bed. The drunk is talking earnestly to the doctor. ". . . a wave of depression came over me," the drunk is saying. "I realized that I was powerless — hopeless — that I couldn't help myself, and that nobody else could help me. I was in black despair. And in the midst of this, I remembered about this God business. . . and I rose up in bed and said, 'If there be a God, let him show himself now!' "

(A doctor specializing in alcoholism hears all kinds of crazy stories from drunks in all stages of de-fogging. You'd expect him to have his tongue in his cheek at this point.)

"All of a sudden, there was a light," the drunk goes on, "a blinding white light that filled the whole room. A tremendous wind seemed to be blowing all around me and right through me. I felt as if I were standing on a high mountain top. . ."

(You'd think a doctor would become hardened after listening to these drunks rave day after day. It's a discouraging, thankless field . . . alcoholism.)

The drunk continued: "I felt that I stood in the presence of God. I felt an immense joy. And I was sure beyond all doubt that I was free from my obsession with alcohol. The only condition was that I share the secret of this freedom with other alcoholics and help them to recover."

The drunk paused and turned to the doctor. "Ever since it happened, I've been lying here wondering whether or not I've lost my mind. Tell me, doctor — am I insane — or not?"

The drunk was Bill W.

Fortunately for Bill — fortunately for AA — fortunately for the thousands of us who have come after—the doctor was Dr. Silkworth. By great good luck — or by the grace of God (depending on your viewpoint) — the doctor was Dr. Silkworth.

It would have been so easy to dismiss Bill's experience as hallucination, one of the many possible vagaries of a rum-soaked brain. And a disparaging word from the doctor right at this point could have choked off the tender shoot of faith and killed it. Alcoholics Anonymous might have got started somewhere else, somehow. Or it might not. Certainly it wouldn't have started here. Very possibly the life of every one of us AAs hung on the doctor's answer to the question, "Am I insane?"

It was here that Dr. Silkworth made the first of his indispensible contributions to AA. He knew — by an insight that no amount of medical training alone can give a man — that what had happened to Bill was real, and important. "I don't know what you've got," he told Bill, "but whatever it is, hang on to it. You are not insane. And you may have the answer to your problem." The encouragement of the man of science, as much as the spiritual experience itself, started AA on its way.

When Dr. Silkworth died of a heart attack in his home in New York early in the morning of March 22nd, even those AAs who knew him best and loved him most awoke to the realization that we had lost a greater friend, a greater doctor, a greater man than we had ever realized. It was particularly hard to appreciate the greatness of the man while Dr. Silkworth was yet with us, because of his profound personal modesty and the disarming gentleness, the unassuming and almost invisible skill, with which he accomplished his daily miracles of medical and spiritual healing.

We knew that he was a prodigious and relentless worker, but still it was a shock to discover that in his lifetime of work with those who suffer our disease, he had talked with 51,000 alcoholics — 45,000 at Towns Hospital and 6,000 at Knickerbocker!

Yet he was never in a hurry. And he had no "formulas," no stock answers. Somehow he found out very early that the unexpected was to be expected in alcoholism, and for a man who knew as many of the answers as he did, he came to each new case with a wonderfully open mind . . . the great and classic example of which is his handling of Bill.

And this gentle little doctor, with his white hair and his china blue eyes — child's eyes, saint's eyes — was a man of immense personal courage. It must be remembered that he went much farther than merely encouraging Bill's faith in his spiritual experience. He saw to it that Bill was permitted to come back into Towns Hospital to share his discovery with other alcoholics. Today — when "carrying the message to others" has become a very respectable part of an undeniably effective program — it is easy to forget that "carrying the message" in the beginning was a highly unorthodox undertaking. It had no precedent and no history of success; most authorities would have turned thumbs down on it as just plain screwball.

Again, we forget how our technique has been mellowed and refined by the wisdom of experience. We know now that the blinding light and the overwhelming rush of God-consciousness are not necessary, that they are indeed very rare phenomena and that the great majority of recoveries among us are of the much less spectacular gradual and educational kind. But in the beginning, the "hot flash" was stressed — nay, insisted upon.

Dr. Silkworth had his professional reputation to lose, and nothing whatsoever to gain, by permitting and encouraging this unheard-of procedure of one God-bitten drunk trying to pass on his strange story of a light and a vision to other alcoholics — most of whom at that time received it with lively hostility or magnificent indifference.

Then Bill met Dr. Bob, and the first few drunks, incredulously, began to make their incredible recoveries. The infant society, without a book, without a program really, and without reputation or standing of any kind — began its growth. We forget how halting and feeble that early growth was, how bedevilled with obstacles in a world skeptical of spiritual experience and often hostile to it.

Dr. Silkworth from the beginning threw all of his weight as a doctor, a neurologist, a specialist in alcoholism, into aiding the progress of this mongrel and highly unpedigreed society in every possible way. He committed social and professional heresy right and left in order to publish and implement his burning faith in a movement which as yet only half-suspected its own destiny and which had to grope rather blindly to find terms for its own faith in itself.

When there was need for money to publish the book *Alcoholics Anonymous*, Dr. Silkworth used his personal influence without stint to help raise the money. As a preface to the book, he wrote the chapter titled, "The Doctor's Opinion," giving AA his praise and approval without reservation or qualification — at a time when there were only a thin one hundred of us dried up!

He was indeed our first friend, and indeed a friend in need. His faith in us was firmer than our faith in ourselves. Bill says: "Without Silky's help, we never would have got going — or kept going!" Again, his contribution was indispensible.

Why did he do it?

The answer to that is the answer to Dr. Silkworth's whole career: he loved drunks. Why he loved drunks is a secret known only to God and the doctor — and perhaps the doctor himself did not wholly understand the mystery. "It's a gift," he used to say, his eyes twinkling.

He discovered his gift very early in his medical practice. He was graduated from Princeton in 1896, and took his medical degree at New York University in 1900. Then he interned at Bellevue; and it was while working at Bellevue that he found he was drawn to alcoholics, and they to him.

When nobody else could calm a disturbed drunk, Dr. Silkworth could. And he found, rather to his amazement, that even the toughest and most case-hardened of drunks would talk to him freely—and that many of them, even more amazingly, wept. It became evident that he exerted — or that there was exerted through him — some kind of thawing influence on the frozen life-springs of the alcoholic.

Yet the years that followed were full of discouragement. There were two years on the psychiatric staff at the U.S. Army Hospital at Plattsburg, New York during the first world war, followed by several years on the staff of the Neurological Institute of the Presbyterian Hospital in New York. Twice he entered into private practice, only to be drawn back into hospital work with alcoholics. His work continued on at Charles B. Towns Hospital, New York, a private hospital specializing in alcoholism and drug addiction. Here, Dr. Silkworth's special skill with alcoholics — and his growing understanding and love for them — had full scope. Yet he estimated that the percentage of real recoveries among the alcoholics he worked with was only about 2 percent. The large number of hopeless cases, and the deep degrees of human tragedy and suffering involved, weighed heavily upon the gentle doctor. He was often profoundly discouraged.

Then came Bill — and AA.

One who has known the doctor intimately over many years has said this about it: "Silky never told me this. It's my own opinion. But I believe that AA was Silky's reward. All those years he plodded along — treating drunks medically — defending them — loving them — and not getting anywhere much. And then God said: 'All right, little man, I'm going to give you and your drunks a lift!' And when the lightning struck, there was Silky, right where he belonged—in the midst of it!"

Early in his career, at a time when alcoholism was almost universally regarded as a willful and deliberate persistence in a nasty vice, Dr. Silkworth came to believe in the essential goodness of the alcoholic. "These people do not want to do the things they do," he insisted. "They drink compulsively, against their will." One of the early drunks whom Dr. Silkworth treated, a big husky six-footer, dropped on his knees before the doctor, tears streaming down his face, begging for a drink. "I said to myself then and there," Dr. Silkworth related, " — this is not just a vice or a habit. This is compulsion, this is pathological craving, this is disease!"

He loved drunks — but there was nothing in the least degree fatuous or sentimental about that love. It could be an astringent love, an almost surgical love. There was the warmest of light in those blue eyes, but still they could burn right through to the bitter core of any lie, any sham. He could see clean through egotism, bombast, self-pity and similar miserable rags that we drunks use so cleverly to hide our central fear and shame.

All this he did — without hurting anyone. While insisting rigorously that recovery was possible only on a moral basis — "You cannot go two ways on a one-way street" — he never preached, never denounced, never even really criticized. He brought you, somehow, to make your own judgments of yourself, the only kind of judgments that count with an alcoholic. How did he do it? "It's a gift." Just coming into his presence was like walking into light. He not only had vision — he gave vision.

There is not room here — nor has there been opportunity for the necessary research — to consider his status as a medical man. It can be said that he held a position of very high eminence in his profession. He encountered opposition to some of his views, and he was latterly the recipient of very widespread recognition and praise for his work. It is literally true that he was the world's greatest practical authority on alcoholism. His pioneering work in the concept of alcoholism as a manifestation of allergy has been validated by later experience and has been the subject of a great deal of medical interest and research just recently.

Dr. Silkworth's was a great contribution to the establishment and development of the alcoholic treatment center at Knickerbocker Hospital in New York. In later years, he was sought out for consultation and advice by doctors and by those in charge of state and city alcoholic treatment projects. There was a steady stream of visitors, some of them from foreign lands. Also, every day, there were long distance telephone calls from those seeking further help, those seeking his advice — all over the U.S.

There remain these things to be noted: Dr. Silkworth was a small man, well under medium height. His complexion was ruddy. His remarkable eyes have been mentioned. His hair was snow white — and no member of AA knew him otherwise, for he was already well along in years when our relationship began. You would say that the habitual expression of his face was a smile — until you thought about it, and realized that the features were really nearly always in repose, and the impression of a smile arose actually from a certain light about his face. (Too many of us have noticed it to be mistaken!)

He loved to be well-dressed — was, in fact, quite dapper — and in this he was not without a certain whimsical and self-recognized vanity. Nurses — the hospital staff — everyone who worked with him quite plainly and simply adored him. He was unfailingly gentle, courteous, thoughtful. He was happily married, and he and Mrs. Silkworth shared a delight in growing things — in flowers — in gardening.

He was utterly and completely indifferent to money, to position, to personal gain or prestige of any kind.

He was a saintly man.

We drunks can thank Almighty God that such a man was designated by the divine Providence to inspire and guide us, individually and as a group, on the long way back to sanity.

And now — in this anonymously written journal of an anonymous society — I hope I may be permitted, in closing, the anomaly of a personal note. You see, Dr. Silkworth saved my life. I was one of those "hopeless" ones whom he reached and brought back to life — to AA — and to God. And I have wanted very much to write this tribute faithfully and well, in the name of all those who share my debt and my gratitude. And yet I have realized from the beginning that this article will entirely please nobody. To those who knew and loved him it will seem insufficient. And some of those who didn't know him may think it overdone, for the truth about Dr. Silkworth is strong medicine in a materialistic age.

This dilemma would be tolerable, were not for a third difficulty: I have written all along in the uneasy knowledge that what is said here is by no means pleasing to the doctor himself. The incident of physical death certainly has not placed him beyond knowledge of what goes on here below. And he will not be pleased with all this, because while he was stern about very few things, he was sternly and seriously opposed to the publication of his own and fame.

I take comfort, however, in the fact that his sense of humor most certainly will have survived his recent transition to a New Home. And I feel sure that his disapproval of the present essay will be tempered by amusement, and by the priceless gift he gave us all so freely while he was yet as we are — his great love.

Anonymous
May 1951

~~~

Section Six

Crossing All Boundaries

In October 1959, Bill W. wrote of his first trip to visit AA abroad and the questions he had about the Fellowship's ability to cross all the obstacles that "divided and shattered the world of our time." He wondered, "Could AA really and fully transcend all of those formidable barriers of race, language, religion, and culture; all of those scars of wars, recent and ancient; all of those kinds of pride and prejudice of which we knew we had our share in America?"

And in answer, he wrote, "As we journeyed from land to land, it was the same everywhere . . . It was so much more than minds cordially meeting minds; it was no simple and merely interesting comparison of mutual experiences and aspirations. This was much, much more; this was the forming of heart to heart in wonder, in joy, and in everlasting gratitude. Lois and I then knew that AA could circle the globe — and it has!"

⤳

The Journey to Kazakhstan

A missionary organization called me, wanting my help. "Yes, we know you aren't the missionary type, but we need someone who knows something about alcoholism." As a sober member of AA and a professional in the treatment field, this was an area where I might be of service. I sat at lunch and heard their story of mission work in the former Soviet satellite country of Kazakhstan. A poor and struggling nation in Central Asia, Kazakhstan had many woes — one of which was a huge problem of alcoholism and drug addiction. A Catholic priest had helped start a small AA meeting in the city of Karaganda, but it was struggling with many slippers. Would I consider going to this remote place to carry the message?

I was intrigued — until I learned it would cost me more than $3,000 to travel there. I apologized, but after all, I had four kids, one entering college. I figured that was the end of it.

Then I attended the AA International Conference in Minneapolis — my first, despite nearly twenty-nine years of sobriety. We gathered in the stadium for the flag ceremony. As I watched the flags appear in alphabetical order, we came to the letter "K." No flag for Kazakhstan. I began to weep. I thought of the many thousands of frivolous dollars I'd spent on my life, only to begrudge my suffering alcoholic friends in Kazakhstan a few bucks. I called when I got home: "I'm going."

Travel to Kazakhstan is arduous, a full three hours east of Moscow by plane. It was truly a trip into another world, an impoverished post-Soviet nation where the average wage is sixty dollars a month. We arrived with four duffel bags that were packed with Big Books in Russian translation paid for by AA members and other friends. We divided the bags among us to get through customs, since we were told Kazakhstan officials routinely confiscate written materials as contraband.

Thus began a two-week journey through the Eurasian steppe, from Petropavlosk (where Solzhenitsyn wrote *The Gulag Archipelego*) to Astana, the capitol. Our itinerary took us to public meetings, two universities, and numerous treatment centers — bleak hospitals that hearkened back to American mental hospitals of the 1930s. Sometimes I chaired two or three meetings a day.

I will never forget the experience of going into alcoholic hospitals with a bag of Russian Big Books, sharing the message of recovery, then passing out the books as gifts to the patients. These men and women were hungry for recovery, and received the books with great gratitude. Coming back the next day and seeing the looks on their faces was indescribable. Even through translators, I could see men and women move from despair to skepticism to hope. Sometimes one would approach me and ask for extra books for alcoholics who were too sick to come to the day room.

I met the small band of alcoholics and their spouses who had, a few months before we arrived, founded AA group number one in Karaganda, Kazakhstan. They were so moved to see a "real" member of AA—and I was equally moved to see these extraordinary folks cradling with reverence a single, battered Russian Big Book. And they had each other. There were tears on both sides as we shared our common problem and our experience, strength, and hope.

These people, alcoholics and professionals alike, had never met an alcoholic who had stayed sober with any lasting success. I was a walking miracle to many of them, more so after I qualified myself with my story. I began to imagine what life in the United States had been like before Bill and Bob met — when hopeless stays in sanitariums were the norm, and alcoholics were viewed as doomed people.

We helped start eight AA meetings in four cities and introduced the newly recovering men and women to the treatment centers so they could make Twelfth Step calls. We talked at length about the Traditions (which are not yet translated into Russian but are much needed). We ate dinner in their homes, laughed, and cried.

On the night before we left, there was a public meeting at the old, crumbling Communist Hall. The event was billed in the paper as a "sober American alcoholic" telling his story. I will never give another open talk like it. There were two hundred and fifty men and women — battered alcoholics and old babushkas in house dresses. They were so desperate.

After I spoke, their homegrown Lois W., a woman named Ludmilla, took the family members back to the auditorium for Kazakhstan's first open Al-Anon meeting. I invited any alcoholics who wished to stay and get a Big Book to come up front. More than seventy-five men and women clamored forward, hopeful that their answer was in this one book. And I knew that the answer was there for them — and in each other.

I recently received word that Kazakhstan's AA group number one celebrated its second anniversary. In all four cities, alcoholics are finding sobriety — and each other. It is slow going, but the process has begun.

It is my prayer that in Toronto in 2005, or at some future International Convention, the opening ceremony will include the lovely blue flag of Kazakhstan. For thirty-one years I have been privileged to receive the many benefits of being a member of Alcoholics Anonymous, but none have been greater than having been of some small service in this foreign land.

Anonymous
Ann Arbor, Michigan
September 2003

∽

Interview: A Door Opens in the People's Republic of China

In August 2001, AA's class A (nonalcoholic) trustee Dr. George Vaillant and two members of the General Service Office were invited to the People's Republic of China to talk about alcoholism and AA. It was the first time representatives of our Fellowship were invited to share their experience, strength, and hope with the medical establishment there and with the pioneers of AA in China who held the first meeting less than a year and a half ago. To find out more about this historic trip, the Grapevine talked with the general manager of GSO. Here are the highlights of that interview.

GV: How did your visit to the People's Republic of China come about?

GM: It was wonderful because it was grounded in the spirit of the Twelfth Step. A few years ago, a group from San Francisco's central office started making trips to Beijing, where they went to expatriot meetings and to hospitals to make contact with patients. And a psychologist from Connecticut who often traveled to China on business had done the same thing.

Those early visits led to the San Francisco members' inviting four psychiatrists from Beijing — Dr. Guizhen Liu from Shandong and Guo Song, Dr. Li Bing, and Dr. Wang Qing Mei from Beijing — to AA's International Convention in Minneapolis, where they met Eva S., the staff person working on AA's General Service Office's international assignment.

When these doctors saw all those sober people in Minneapolis and the celebration of the spirit there, they said, Gee, we need more information. So they arranged, through Dr. Yucan Shen, a member of the World Health Organization and one of China's foremost physicians,

119

to invite our class A trustee Dr. George Vaillant to lecture at hospitals in Beijing and Changchun. And Eva and I were invited to tag along.

GV: What were these doctors' impressions of AA at that point?

GM: They told us that they started reading about Alcoholics Anonymous seven years ago and got very curious about its success rate. Before that, they had experienced defeat after defeat trying to help their patients maintain abstinence from alcohol. The patients would do fine as long as they were in the psychiatric wards, but as soon as they got on the streets, they relapsed. The doctors were frustrated by their inability to help these alcoholics.

Then, shortly after they returned from Minneapolis, Dr. Song and Dr. Bing began to hold AA meetings in their psychiatric wards, and lo and behold, the patients were staying sober. We arrived just after the Easy in Sobriety group that Guo Song started at Beijing Anding Hospital celebrated its first anniversary.

These doctors are students of AA, really visionaries. AA World Services has approved translations of AA literature into Mandarin and Simplified Chinese [which bridges China's different dialects], and they have read quite a lot of it. And through that literature they have been able to see that AA is a resource for treating alcoholism in their country. They have embraced it as a solution.

GV: Some people were concerned that the Chinese government would view a visit like this as an intrusion from the West, an attempt to import Western values. Was that a problem?

GM: We did wonder if we were going to have problems because China is a closed society. But that was not the case at all. We were welcomed with open arms by hospital administrators, by physicians, and members of the press, who were in attendance at all our meetings, and who had tons of questions. (By the way, the doctors had read our Traditions and knew that Dr. Vaillant could be photographed, while Eva and I needed to protect our anonymity.)

The government itself was silent about our visit. But we knew that they were very aware that AA meetings were taking place. And they were aware that several hospitals in other parts of China were starting to embrace the AA model as part of their treatment for alcoholism as well.

I know that government officials sit on the board of directors of one of the hospitals we visited, so the government is aware of AA's birth in their country. One would assume the government's silence is a positive, because we learned from one of the hundreds of medical practitioners who attended Dr. Vaillant's presentations that the Korean fellowship had brought AA into Northern China ten years before and had started several meetings. But eventually something went wrong and the government cracked down and stopped the meetings. So there seems to have been a change in China's official view of AA.

GV: So the literature was vital to carrying the message.

GM: Yes, it's so important. When Bill was writing the Big Book, he envisioned a salesman taking the book throughout the United States and giving it to people as a guide to getting sober, starting AA meetings, and living a spiritual way of life. And so this wonderful story just repeated itself over and over until individual members, whether in the United States or in other countries, became part of this joyful carrying of the message—responsible and joyful. In fact, I participated in a wonderful Twelfth Step experience while I was there.

GV: What happened?

GM: A member of the group at Beijing Anding Hospital named Mr. M., who was instrumental in helping AA get started in Beijing, had been twelve-stepped by his brother several months earlier. But since then, his brother had relapsed and was in the hospital.

GV: In Beijing?

GM: He had gotten sober there, but at the time he was in a hospital in a city called Tianjin. So Eva, I, Mr. M.'s sponsor Brad, who's a U.S. citizen working in China, and a few of our Chinese friends did this wonderful AA Twelfth Step. We all piled into a car and drove two hours from Beijing to the psychiatric hospital in Tianjin, which was down a back street and surrounded by tough living conditions. The administrator of the hospital led us through the hospital, out a back door, and up some stairs to a conference room, which was filled with members of the media! Mr. M. gave a little history of AA in Beijing, the media left, and we started an AA meeting.

Mr. M. and Brad had driven to Tianjin to twelve-step Mr. M.'s brother the week before, so it was only their second meeting. The sharing was in Chinese, but we knew when they were talking about what happened and what it's like now from the body language and of course the translators. It was so wonderful to see Mr. M. thanking his brother for carrying the message to him, and saying, "Now I've brought all of my friends here to carry the message to you, and we hope and pray that you can embrace AA and stay sober as soon as you're released from this hospital."

It was great AA. It was all about giving love and being of service to someone else so that they can have that experience.

GV: And that hope.

GM: Yes. This is why it is so important to go to other countries and share our experience: I drank every day, but when I got sober on Maui, there were seven meetings a week, so I could go to a meeting every day. The people in Beijing have only one meeting a week, and they're having trouble staying sober. They're trying, but they're not.

So we were able to say, "Why don't you have a meeting every day?" "We don't have a place," they'd say. And we'd say, "Meet each other every day on the street corner, have tea, touch base with one another. You need to see and be with each other. Have these AA contacts. Start this fellowship, because it's so important that you talk to one another."

This is the story of Bill and Dr. Bob being repeated, because in fact we were with the founders of AA in China. In thirty or forty years, these men and women will be looked upon as the pioneers of AA in China.

GV: Have you heard whether Mr. M.'s brother has stayed sober?

GM: Yes, he has.

GV: Where else in China did you visit?

GM: Dr. Vaillant helped us organize a meeting in the northern city of Changchun, although it was Eva who set the stage during each one of our visits for us to be with alcoholics.

Dr. Vaillant was invited to the hospital to show Chinese physicians how he gained the patient's confidence and help him see the history of his alcoholism and how the alcohol had turned on him. Then, Dr. Vaillant said, "If we offered you a solution, would you be willing to go to a meeting?" And the patient said, "Yes." And so, with the hospital's approval, we had an AA meeting right there — the first one in Changchun.

GV: How many people were at that meeting?

GM: Four alcoholic patients, Dr. Wright, Dr. Lee Bing, and three patients' wives. The news media were there, too, and they listened quietly.

GV: Why was the media present almost everywhere you went?

GM: Having someone of Dr. Vaillant's stature visit China was an important event for them. He is a distinguished psychiatrist and his book on alcoholism and the usage of Alcoholics Anonymous as a model for helping alcoholics is world famous.

I also think the doctors in China wanted to promote AA as a resource. For so many years, they've been frustrated by not being able to help these sick and dying alcoholics. Now they have a solution and they really want to share it.

GV: AA presents the people of China with such a different way of thinking. Did they have any difficulty accepting it?

GM: We were very curious how the Big Book would be interpreted and whether it would be embraced. We were particularly concerned about two aspects of the Big Book: first and foremost was the use of the word God. And although we're very clear that we're a spiritual fellowship and that we embrace all religions, all spiritual ideas, we thought people brought up in China might have some difficulties with translating the idea of a Higher Power into their culture and accepting it.

We were surprised that they didn't have trouble at all. They interpreted the Higher Power as heaven. Believing in a power greater than themselves was natural for them. So that wasn't the difficulty.

The difficulty was really the translation of the word anonymous and the concept of anonymity.

We had discovered that in Japan, being anonymous is viewed as being secret, or keeping something to one's self. So Japanese AAs get an alias, and that is the name they use.

GV: A code name.

GM: We believe that may hinder their ability to go to the public and the professional community and let them know that AA is a resource. It may also hinder them in helping to change their society's view of alcoholism as a disease rather than as a stigma. We thought members of the Fellowship in China might have a similar problem. So after many discussions, it was suggested that Alcoholics Anonymous be translated as Alcoholics Unknown in China, which seemed very acceptable to the alcoholics there.

GV: In your travel report, you describe your trip to China as "a mountain-top experience." What did you mean by that?

GM: It's the experience of sitting across from a man who has been locked up in a psychiatric ward for quite a while — a man with a scar from ear to ear that he got trying to slit his own throat because he could not stop drinking. It is looking him in the eyes and sharing as one alcoholic with another and seeing that glimmer of hope, that little flicker of light go on, and knowing that I, we, and AA here in the United States, had some little part in changing this man. It is believing a seed has been planted in him and that will grow and grow.

It reaffirmed how blessed I am to be able to take the experience we've gathered here in the United States and share it with others. That's the mountain-top experience.

February 2002

୬

AA Under the Moon and Stars

**Elaine McDowell, Nonalcoholic Chair of the General Service Board in
the U.S. and Canada, Talks About the Growth of AA in Cameroon**

*AA has been flourishing in South Africa for more than fifty years. It is now tak-
ing root in Cameroon and other countries on the African continent. Late last
fall, Dr. Elaine McDowell, PhD, chair of the AA General Service Board, U.S.
and Canada; a French-speaking GSO staff member; and the chair and two staff
members of the French General Service Board traveled to Cameroon to share
how the general service structures in their countries support AA groups and
their Twelfth-Step work. To learn more about this historic journey, the
Grapevine interviewed Dr. McDowell during a recent General Service Board
weekend. This is the story of their trip to Cameroon.*

GV: Can you tell us more about the purpose of the trip?

EM: AA groups in Cameroon have spread very quickly; however,
there was no service structure to support them, so they invited the
French and the Americans to share their experiences in developing a
service structure. This was the principal purpose for going to
Cameroon.

GV: About how many AA members are there in Cameroon?

EM: The number that is tossed about is 2,000 AA members. As in
the United States, we don't know the exact number. This is an esti-
mate.

GV: Are these AAs from the Cameroon-born population or primarily
Europeans living abroad?

EM: They are primarily Cameroons. Do you know the history?

GV: No. I would love to hear it.

EM: There was a prison guard named Donatien B. working in a jail
in Monatele, a village outside of Yaoundé, the capital. He was an alco-

holic who wanted to get sober but didn't know how to do it. One day, he awoke in a drunken fog to find a piece of AA literature written in French by his bedside. So he got in touch with the French General Service Office, where the information was printed, and they began communicating.

Around the same time, another alcoholic who wanted to get sober also came upon some information about AA. But the AA literature he had was from the Belgian General Service Office, so he got in touch with it. The Belgian General Service Office mentioned him to the French General Service Office, and they said, "Why don't we put these two people together?" So they did, and these two men became the co-founders of AA in Cameroon.

The second man, Jean-Baptiste O., lived in Yaoundé and was soon in touch with Donatien. The French stayed in contact, and they both participated with us in the formation of Cameroon's general service structure.

GV: Did Donatien and Jean-Baptiste speak about their Twelfth-Step experiences in Cameroon?

EM: I don't recall specific information about that except to say that the AA message had such universal appeal to alcoholics in Cameroon that AA groups were quickly formed.

GV: Who else did you meet?

EM: The former Minister of Social Affairs, Dr. Marie Madeleine Fouda, met us at the airport and took us to her home. Home-served meals are an important custom in Cameroon, so we had dinner with her and met some local AA members there. Dr. Fouda is very well known, very well respected, especially for her work with the under-privileged, and she's had a long history of interest in alcoholism. She's very gracious and very committed, with a lot of passion for the program.

GV: What did you do in Cameroon?

EM: Let me tell you: They had a very full schedule for us. There were many public information meetings, and they occurred in several settings. Some were held in community centers. Others were held in hospitals, health clinics, and government offices, and one was at an 8 A.M. Mass at a trustee's church, because Cameroon is heavily Catholic.

Because Dr. Fouda had been a cabinet member, she could open all kinds of doors. We met the Minister of Health, who introduced us to the Director of Alcohol and Drug Abuse, and she, in turn, invited us to visit a health center, where we had a joyful sharing with the professional staff.

Later, we visited the Minister of Corrections and talked with him. Dr. Fouda also arranged meetings with officials we would think of as county executives or mayors. In fact, they have a custom in Cameroon that every outsider is required to visit the local dignitaries before meeting anyone else in the community. Therefore, we followed protocol by touching base with the local officials who would then call a community meeting and have everyone from the village come. So we had different kinds of meetings every day.

GV: Do one or two in particular stand out?

EM: Yes, our visit to the prison where the first AA group in Cameroon met. When we walked through the door, the inmates in AA stood up and started singing a song about the Fellowship. They had put what AA meant to them to music. They performed a skit outdoors, on the ground, in this tremendous heat. They were truly beside themselves with excitement that we had come from America and from France to visit with them inside the prison.

We also had an interesting experience with the corrections official there. "This AA — how do you know it works?" he said to us. "I don't know anyone it has worked for." And Donatien, who does a lot of work with inmates when they're released, said, "It worked for me." "You, you are an alcoholic?" the official exclaimed. "I don't believe it!" "Yes, and I got sober," Donatien said. And the official replied, "Okay. I know this man, and I know what he means to our community, so you have my full support."

GV: That's great.

EM: Another day, we went to a trustee's house to help the Cameroon AAs establish their service structure. We arrived, had our meal, of course, and when we sat down to begin our work, some gentlemen came by, carrying their Big Book, and said, "We were scheduled to have an AA meeting with you." There was some confusion because so many groups wanted us to meet with them. "Well, no," we responded, "we really do have to work on the service structure now." And they were not happy.

So we said, "Why don't you sit down and observe what we're about to do." We had this wonderful meeting, where we shared American and French experiences. I also spent some time talking about *AA Comes of Age,* because it explains that the beginning of AA in the United States, was, in many respects, a matter of trial and error. The Cameroons are going to have some pitfalls and struggles as well, but they can be overcome. We hoped that the history would encourage them to persevere. We shared about our structure, about the kind of contributions nonalcoholic trustees can make, and then we talked about literature distribution. There is a big need for literature in Cameroon, and some type of literature distribution network is needed.

At any rate, as we finally came to the close of the meeting, the gentleman who had wanted an AA meeting said, "You know, I am so happy that I sat here, because we thought that you just wanted to go sightseeing. And this is so important, what you've just done. We've seen history being made here. Thank you for letting us sit in."

GV: What other challenges do alcoholics in Cameroon face?

EM: They have such everyday life challenges, just for food, water, and housing, along with AIDS and other diseases. But in spite of it all, these people have been uplifted by the Fellowship, because sober people who practice the principles of AA are much stronger people spiritually and can do more for themselves and others.

They are also good role models. For instance, when the doctor suggested to one of the alcoholics we were talking with, "Drink a lot of water," he replied, "That's the point. Our water's no good. So we drink the diseased water or we drink alcohol." We were able to say, "You have to talk among yourselves. Ask fellow Cameroons how they got sober. How do they deal with the water situation? Maybe you could do what they're doing."

Their problem is daily sustenance, and that is what really grabs you. You see all of that, and then you see that with AA, they now feel something greater than themselves in terms of being connected to this larger Fellowship. There we were from U.S., Canada, and France, but when we held hands and said the Serenity Prayer, they felt connected. They knew we were one Fellowship and they were part of it. It was great.

AA Under the Moon and Stars

While in Cameroon, Elaine and her group also attended a special AA meeting. Elaine reports:

Donatien's house, where we met to discuss Cameroon's general service structure, was in a remote rural area. When we finished, about six o'clock in the evening, we headed back over unpaved roads toward the main highway. But just as we came to the intersection, this little truck pulled up, and a gentleman jumped out. He turned out to be one of the rural parish priests. And he said, "Mesdames, you can't leave. There are twenty-nine people waiting for you. They have been waiting three hours for an AA meeting." And we said, "Oh, my goodness. We didn't know that. We have to go back." So we turned around and went back into the bush, with the priest leading, traveling on unpaved roads that became curving trails through the mud.

Soon, we began seeing stragglers who had given up on our coming and were heading home. They saw the truck and shouted, "Oh, they're here!" and jumped in the back of the priest's truck. Then we'd go a little further and see more stragglers until there were eleven people in the back of his little truck. When we finally arrived, the others were waiting in this church with a dirt floor and wooden benches.

By this time, it was so dark, we couldn't see to read the Preamble. They'd thought we would come in the day and hadn't brought candles. We were dismayed, thinking we would not be able to have the meeting. But the AA members simply picked up the benches and took them outside. And we had the most magical meeting.

We heard the same stories that you hear here — stories of lost lives and all the desperation of alcoholism. And we heard of the miracles of achieving sobriety and the differences it made in their lives. It was just incredible. A couple of people there were still drinking but wanted to become sober. They asked the doctor, "Can you give me some medication to help me, because I don't want to drink again. I need something. I lost my wife, I lost this, I lost that, and everything is gone. But I don't want to drink again." And she gave them tips about their diet and said, "Keep coming to meetings."

It was so amazing because the moon and the stars were out, and you could start making out faces. I looked up and I thought, Yes, AA is anywhere, everywhere, for anyone who has a desire to stop drinking.

June 2003

✌

Section Seven

Passing It On

The chain reaction of help, healing, and hope at AA's core has generated energy and enthusiasm throughout the Fellowship for over seventy years. Millions have found sobriety and contented, useful lives. Yet how shall we pass this message of hope on to those who will follow? What responsibility do we have to the future of AA?

As Bill W. wrote in the book *AA Today,* published by the Grapevine in July 1960, "Will we continue to search out the ever present flaws and gaps in our communications? With enough imagination, courage, and dedication, will we resolutely address ourselves to those many tasks of repair and improvement which even now the future is calling upon us to undertake? Still clearer vision and an ever mounting sense of responsibility can be the only answers to these questions."

🔊

Pass It On—But How?

It is a paradox that one of the basic tenets of the AA program is that we must give away what we have in order to keep it. In other words, it is necessary to our own sobriety that we share freely with others what we have been so freely given. "When we see a man sinking into the mire that is alcoholism, we give him first aid and place what we have at his disposal" (*Alcoholics Anonymous,* page 132). This has not been seen as optional but necessary to the success of an AA member's program. "Though they knew they must help other alcoholics if they would remain sober. . ." (*Alcoholics Anonymous,* page 159), the giving away also became a pleasure in itself. The necessity of the motive "was transcended by the happiness they found in giving of themselves for others" (*Alcoholics Anonymous,* page 159).

The importance of passing it on is simply stated in our Responsibility Declaration:

"I am responsible. When anyone, anywhere, reaches out for help, I want the hand of AA always to be there. And for that: I am responsible."

The AA Preamble emphasizes the same point, saying we are "men and women who share their experience, strength and hope with each other that they may solve their common problem and help others to recover from alcoholism." Tradition Five states that "our Society has concluded it has but one high mission — to carry the AA message to those who don't know there's a way out" ("Twelve and Twelve," page 151).

Our whole meeting structure is based on this concept, our literature works toward this end, and good-spirited AA members through the years have contributed to this stream of continuity with each passing the message on to others and variously helping his fellows along the "Road of Happy Destiny."

But how are we to do this in new times to come? Various experiments and changes were made in the history of AA, and some have developed into generally consistent methods of operation. The Traditions give us our basic guideposts. For example: Tradition Four gives groups the right to individualize some things, but Tradition Three seems to curtail such innovations as the membership requirements indicated by the Little Rock Plan (*The Home Group,* pages 66–68). Generally speaking, the Traditions developed over time in response to problems as they developed, and as such give us a tried and true guide to operate, while still allowing individualization.

Over time, however, people do change in their very approach to AA. In the six decades or so since Bill W. worked with his early prospects, there have been many changes, and many more likely to come in the next century. In particular, two very pertinent changes have already altered the work of AA and seem likely to continue as relative to AA. Years ago, nearly any person would publicly profess religion and willingly seek divine help in "taking the pledge" in order to free himself from the demon alcohol. However, as the public has become more enlightened about the addictive and progressive aspects of alcoholism as a disease instead of a demon, the public has become likewise noticeably less religious.

In the early part of the century, alcoholic drinking was shameful and religion almost a matter of course. In today's world, there are many people who are perhaps put off by or even embarrassed by religiosity, who may nonetheless take a rather enlightened point of view about the disease of alcoholism. While alcoholism is still seen by the general public as a regrettable circumstance, it does not generally warrant the shame and scandal it did then. On the other hand, religion itself may now carry with it for many people a certain stigma and certainly produce a substantial hindrance to many modern people. This "modernization" is likely to increase and as such is bound to affect a program that seems to rely on the one trait to assist in the recovery from the other.

It would seem to me that many of us now in AA have felt the various calls for good sense, for will power, and for religion, and nonetheless remained doomed and hopeless and in need of a solution. If focus is needed to direct AA's course of action into the new century it should be one that avoids frills and frivolities and concentrates on the basics. We may take advantage of new technologies, make changes from time to time as is deemed wise at those times, and we may thoroughly enjoy ourselves. But we must remain focused on the simple basics as we move into the future. We must not lose track of those basics no matter what the future holds.

The last words of the Preamble say it clearly: "Our primary purpose is to stay sober and help other alcoholics to achieve sobriety."

Charlie R.
Athens, Georgia
January 2000

ᔥ

You're Needed Here

I am black, female, and alcoholic. Before AA, I often considered those facts a rather tragic and unfair cross to bear. Today, these self-same realities assure me that I have both purpose and responsibility. My responsibility to all alcoholics, sober and active, male and female, black, brown, yellow, red and white is beyond question. However, the additional, and perhaps special, purpose that my Higher Power may see fit to use me for is, in my view, related to the fact that I am first a black alcoholic and second a female alcoholic.

Like many of you, I'm sure, I walked into the rooms of AA with my head bowed, consumed by so much shame that I could hardly look anyone in the eye. Sure, I heard your attempts to reassure me. "Alcoholism is a disease," you said. But for me it was an intolerable disgrace that I was convinced had been foolishly inflicted upon me by my own hand. Thus, self-flagellation was a regular and daily occurrence. At meetings, I noticed every gesture, every word, that in my distorted view of things validated and justified my intense self-loathing. One thing I noticed was that I saw few alcoholics who looked like me — black and female. This absence deepened my feeling of being "different" and alone.

One day, still in that first painful year of early sobriety, Charlotte came into my life. Charlotte was about ten years sober at the time, black, beautiful (inside and out), and totally devoted to the Fellowship and program of Alcoholics Anonymous. I'll never forget Charlotte's response to my timidly asked question: "Are there fewer black women alcoholics than other alcoholics?"

Charlotte smiled at me knowingly, as if my question was perfectly normal, and, more importantly, as if she knew and understood that painful place from which my opinion originated. "No, I don't think there are fewer, but I do think that some may come, look around, not identify and leave, and that many others just haven't gotten here yet."

Charlotte then said something that absolutely altered my perspective in AA and helped me to begin the process of not so much letting go of the feeling of being different, but embracing my difference as a God-given blessing. Charlotte said, "You're needed here. You need to be in the rooms for the ones who may need to identify with you, for the ones that haven't gotten here yet." It was at this moment that what I thought was a tragedy began to be revealed to me as a blessing.

The responsibility that I have felt in being black, female, and alcoholic hasn't always been easy. But AA has taught me how to be responsible, and through practicing the principles of our program, the Twelve Steps, Twelve Traditions, and Twelve Concepts, I believe I have grown in my ability to handle this responsibility. I have tried to be sensitive to the need we have in AA to demonstrate that Alcoholics Anonymous is for all alcoholics. There are those who may argue that there really isn't anything that needs to be done to affirm this fact. I disagree. I have learned several other things from "old-timers" in AA about how to increase the probability that our message of "inclusion for all alcoholics" gets through. Some of the things I have learned are: 1) If I am given the privilege of choosing AA speakers for meetings, workshops, conventions, etc., I should be sensitive in my selections so that there is representation on the level of different races, sexes, age groups, etc.; 2) When sponsoring newcomers, I can pass on what I have learned in this area to increase their sensitivity; 3) I can speak up about this issue even though it may be uncomfortable, unpopular, or not well-received; 4) I can sponsor newcomers from underrepresented groups into service.

At our 55th International Convention, I attended a workshop on the historical perspective of blacks in AA. Listening to "what it was like in our past histories," when in certain parts of the United States blacks weren't allowed even to drink coffee after the meetings, certainly filled me with gratitude for how it is. But looking at how it is, both the progress that we've made and the areas where we still grow, fills me with hope, inspiration, and a resolve to do my part in carrying the message of AA to all alcoholics in the spirit of the Third Tradition that AA may never exclude, overtly or covertly, any alcoholic who may need our help.

Dorothy H.
Piscataway, New Jersey
July 1991

ॐ

How Others See Us

At a recent meeting, a woman who'd been sober for some time asked the question, "Why do we close with the Lord's Prayer if we are not a Christian organization?" This, of course, spawned lengthy discussion, both pro and con, on an increasingly divisive issue:

what should be AA's relationship to this traditionally Christian prayer?

It is a question I've struggled with on a personal level for years. I am a Buddhist and an agnostic, and at times have found the prayer offensive. At other times, I have been successful in "translating" the prayer into terms comfortable for me. These days, I join in the closing prayer with everyone else, content to "stop fighting anyone or anything." Yet the discussion at this meeting made me take another look at the prayer and my own relationship to it.

The Lord's Prayer is unique among the prayers used in AA meetings. It does not appear in the Big Book, yet it is the most common closing prayer at meetings in the United States. And, unlike the Serenity, Third Step, and Seventh Step prayers, it appears in the Biblical Gospels, and is therefore inherently linked with Christianity.

I have heard AA members argue that the prayer is nonetheless "universal." This is difficult to accept. I believe the original prayer was written by a rabbi in the first century BC, but it was adopted by Jesus and given to his earliest followers, and seems to have been abandoned by rabbinic Judaism — most Jews I know believe the prayer to be Christian. Because of centuries of missionary activity, this prayer is seen as a hallmark of Christianity by Christians and non-Christians alike. In India, AA members in meetings I went to did not say it because they don't believe that God is a "father who art in heaven," nor that his kingdom is coming — that is a uniquely Christian idea. At least one of the world's religions — my own — does not even believe in God. For more than half the world's population, this "universal" prayer poses serious problems.

I've heard people say things like, "Well, if they really want to get sober, they'll come anyway," or "I didn't believe in God when I came in, and I got sober." I used to be accepting of such positions. Then I spent two months in Chiang Mai, Thailand, where they have great AA meetings. I was glad to see that the Steps had been translated into Thai, since alcoholism is a terrible problem in northern Thailand. But during my stay, I didn't see a single Thai member or newcomer attend the group — it was all expatriates. When I asked one of the members about this, he told me it was a problem with language. It seems the Thai language has several words for God. The one chosen for translation of the Steps was a word associated by the Thais with Christianity. Thailand is ninety-five percent Buddhist, and resisted Christian missionary attempts for centuries. AA's perceived association with Christianity is culturally offensive to them, and very few Thais get sober.

This is not an issue of individual religious stubbornness. Imagine, for a moment, if AA in the United States opened with a reading by Marx or Lenin. Many Americans would be confronted by a philosophy that they opposed all their lives. They may have gone to war, they may have lost family members in the struggle against it. To accept it would not only violate their own beliefs, but would open them to scorn and ostracism from society. How many would stay? How many would choose to die rather than give in — assuming that, as confused as newcomers can be, they were aware that death by alcoholism was their only alternative?

Let us be clear about one thing: the AA program works, even for Buddhists. It is not necessary to become Christian, or even to believe in God in the traditional western sense. My own sobriety is proof of that. But to publicly use a prayer which is seen by many as an overt symbol of Christianity is to deny millions the opportunity to try. Even here in the United States, which is still predominantly Christian, pluralism is increasing through immigration and conversion. The number of non-Christians needing AA is increasing, too.

The issue is not whether the Lord's Prayer is or is not Christian—that is open to debate. The issue is, rather, that much of the world perceives the Lord's Prayer as being Christian—a fact difficult to argue with.

I've made my peace with the prayer on a personal level, but I also have a responsibility to speak my conscience to the group. I hope that by increasing our awareness of how other cultures and religions see us, AA's effectiveness can also be increased.

Alcoholism cuts across religious lines. Perhaps someday AA truly will as well.

D. J. M.

Los Angeles, California

May 1999

༽

Keeping Recovery Alive

I serve as an area Archivist from the Southeast Region. Archivists tend to look back. We reminisce, we wander, we wonder, we collect "old things." And so recently I began to wander back in time: AA's time and my time.

My wandering made me think of my grandmother who, in December 1899, must have been wondering about the baby she was going to have. On January 4, 1900, her third child and first girl (my mother) came into this world. I never asked my grandmother if she wondered about the new century. She never knew that her only granddaughter became an alcoholic. Four years after her death I found a life of sobriety in Alcoholics Anonymous. I like to think she would be happy for me. My mother wasn't. For most of my drinking life, she said, "You drink too much" and when I joined AA she said, "You're not that bad."

Lately I've been wandering back to my early AA meetings. My first home group was a discussion group — one of the earliest discussion groups in the area where I found the Fellowship. I remember the criticism and clucking the old-timers were doing: "A speaker meeting is good enough for us. Why not them?" Today, in my part of the country, speaker meetings are few and far between and discussion groups the norm. After twenty-four years of sobriety that I don't take credit for, I too criticize and cluck at these young newcomers. They have new ideas, different outside needs and interests. And I ask myself — how can Alcoholics Anonymous survive? For nearly sixty-five years we have kept alive our recovery and passed it on to those who came through our doors. Can today's newcomers pass on the wisdom of sixty-five years of a program so unique most of the world doesn't even have a speaking acquaintance with it?

In my beginnings, we didn't read "How It Works," the Twelve Traditions, the Promises, or anything at the start of our meetings. The Serenity Prayer and the Lord's Prayer were used. No chanting took place, and if anyone had grabbed my sweaty hands, I'd have cussed them out. So I ask myself, Is this a good change or a bad change? In all my wisdom I have to say — I don't know. But changes come. One good change is that today we have lots of Step meetings; they are so important to me. When I came in, we had no Step meetings.

I was watching a morning news program the other day. Some folks were gathering items for a time capsule. I said to my husband, "I wonder if AA will go in there? And if it does, what's going to happen when, in the next millennium, someone opens it and says, 'AA — is that some fly-by-night group that no longer exists?' Or will they say, 'Wow! In 1935 a couple of old sots began staying sober and even today, January 2100, old and young sots are finding a life of sobriety and serenity!' "

In my home group, which is thirty-five years old, we have an elder statesman who is one of the founders of the group and has watched the group grow and change. He brings forty-two years of sobriety to our meetings. I continually marvel at him when I watch him at business meetings. Some of the ideas and suggestions (some in the form of rules) that come along must seem ludicrous to him. Yet he hardly ever speaks against something or for something unless asked for his experience. But he is always there for the group and anyone else who needs help.

How did AA affect my life when I first got here, as opposed to how it affects people today? The first time I came to an AA meeting, I was ready for a new life. Somehow I knew when you came to AA you didn't drink. I have a sponsee today who figures it is all right to have a glass of wine now and then! I'm sure she is in the minority — I hope. When I first heard about high bottoms and low bottoms, I was sure I was a high-bottom drunk. The longer I stay around, the more I realize that I was a pretty low-bottom drunk. My sponsee only drinks now and then, but when she does, she really makes a mess of things. But she can't see that yet. So, do I give her the same kind of help I got, or do I take a different approach? I'll probably be a little softer with her. Maybe less aggressive. This I do know, the God of my understanding will show the way as he has since I first came around. So the approach will probably be this: here it is — my experience, strength, and hope.

The original speaker meetings are so important to me too.

So will AA survive in the new millennium? I don't know, but this I do know: if we follow our Traditions, we will survive and, I hope, grow. The Traditions tell us to serve — not govern; to attract — not promote; to carry the message — not force it on anyone; to keep the three legacies alive: recovery, unity, and service. These I truly believe are our lifelines.

As of this writing, I am seventy-one years young. I do fear that maybe someday one of my eleven grandchildren will need this Fellowship, and it will have been so watered down that it will be useless to them. Then I remember: in 1935, there would have been no hope for me or them. So I pray that AA will be here for me, and those I love, and those I don't know yet.

I think it will.

Anonymous
Raleigh, North Carolina
January 2000

◈

We Who Are Next in Line

I am a twenty-two-year-old alcoholic. After several years of hard
drinking, I was dying of alcoholism. Doctors had told me I was
incurable and hopeless. I began to recover through the program of
Alcoholics Anonymous, and by the grace of a very loving God and AA
I'm still sober three years later. Because of my recovery, I was allowed
to pursue a lifelong dream and I enlisted in the Air Force. This has
given me the opportunity to attend AA meetings in different states
and other nations, and I have noticed something interesting in my
travels. Where a meeting allows people to talk about drug addiction, it
usually allows them to talk about everything else under the sun and
they invariably do. In these meetings that have little regard for AA
Traditions, there seem to be more people who go back to drinking,
more people who don't practice the Twelve Steps, more people who
don't have (or don't use) a sponsor, more people who don't extend a
safe welcome to visitors or pay much attention to newcomers.

However, on the other side of the coin, meetings that insist on
discussing subjects related to recovery from alcoholism only — and
stand by it — are often meetings that make sure a new person is
welcomed and given phone numbers with maybe a pamphlet or two,
meetings that make their visitors feel like they've come home, meetings that get involved with hospitals and institutions committees and
their service centers. These meetings produce a different result. The
old-timers are there, and they have a respected voice because of their
tested experience. People at those meetings have and use sponsors and
they talk about how they've applied the AA program in their daily
lives. They have more solutions and talk less about problems, more
peace and less turmoil, and more people who stay recovered and less
who go back to drinking again.

Bill W. was right: AA cannot fix the world. AA's Twelve Steps and

Traditions can be applied universally to everyone's benefit, but AA itself must forever remain by and for alcoholics. To mix up our primary purpose — freedom from alcohol — with drug addiction and overeating and other destructive dependencies erodes the unity that binds us together, unity we must keep to survive. It's not a matter of exclusivity, it's a matter of the survival of AA's very existence.

Since the Fellowship's early days, we have had the Twelve Steps to guide us. But the bedrock of AA has always been one drunk talking to another. Through this, the depth of understanding is reached that gives hope to a desolate alcoholic's heart. One drunk to another — not one addict to an alcoholic or one codependent to an alcoholic.

One day it will be left to the young people now in our Fellowship to carry on the original spirit and traditions of AA, even though the buzz words and trends will come and go. It will be up to us to teach newcomers how to maintain the type of sobriety that achieves the promises of the Big Book and dispels some of the fables of recovery popular today. It will be up to us to help the newcomer from the street dry out, shakes and pukes and all. We will be left to teach the little things: how to sit at the front, not the back of the room, say hello to the new guy, wash coffee cups and ashtrays. One day it will be up to us to uphold the Traditions. It will be up to us to keep it simple.

Today, young people are learning from the last generation of AAs who got the message straight from the original old-timers. We must be diligent in preserving the AA way of life through our actions and our participation at meetings amid an ever growing attitude of "I come first" rather than "sobriety comes first." There are many catchwords, but only one program of recovery outlined in the Big Book.

Old-timers, there are still some of us who desperately need you and value what you have to say.

Young people, it's our responsibility to follow in their footsteps.

Jenifer C.
Bury St. Edmunds, England
September 1994

The Twelve Steps

1. We admitted we were powerless over alcohol — that our lives had become unmanageable.

2. Came to believe that a Power greater than ourselves could restore us to sanity.

3. Made a decision to turn our will and our lives over to the care of God *as we understood Him.*

4. Made a searching and fearless moral inventory of ourselves.

5. Admitted to God, to ourselves, and to another human being the exact nature of our wrongs.

6. Were entirely ready to have God remove all these defects of character.

7. Humbly asked Him to remove our shortcomings.

8. Made a list of all persons we had harmed, and became willing to make amends to them all.

9. Made direct amends to such people wherever possible, except when to do so would injure them or others.

10. Continued to take personal inventory and when we were wrong promptly admitted it.

11. Sought through prayer and meditation to improve our conscious contact with God as we understood Him, praying only for knowledge of His will for us and the power to carry that out.

12. Having had a spiritual awakening as the result of these steps, we tried to carry this message to alcoholics, and to practice these principles in all our affairs.

The Twelve Traditions

1. Our common welfare should come first; personal recovery depends upon AA unity.

2. For our group purpose there is but one ultimate authority — a loving God as He may express Himself in our group conscience. Our leaders are but trusted servants; they do not govern.

3. The only requirement for AA membership is a desire to stop drinking.

4. Each group should be autonomous except in matters affecting other groups or AA as a whole.

5. Each group has but one primary purpose — to carry its message to the alcoholic who still suffers.

6. An AA group ought never endorse, finance or lend the AA name to any related facility or outside enterprise, lest problems of money, property, and prestige divert us from our primary purpose.

7. Every AA group ought to be fully self-supporting, declining outside contributions.

8. Alcoholics Anonymous should remain forever nonprofessional, but our service centers may employ special workers.

9. AA, as such, ought never be organized; but we may create service boards or committees directly responsible to those they serve.

10. Alcoholics Anonymous has no opinion on outside issues; hence the AA name ought never be drawn into public controversy.

11. Our public relations policy is based on attraction rather than promotion; we need always maintain personal anonymity at the level of press, radio and films.

12. Anonymity is the spiritual foundation of all our traditions, ever reminding us to place principles before personalities.

The AA Grapevine Statement of Purpose

The AA Grapevine is the international journal of Alcoholics Anonymous. Written, edited, illustrated, and read by AA members and others interested in the AA program of recovery from alcoholism, the Grapevine is a lifeline linking one alcoholic to another.

Widely known as a "meeting in print," the AA Grapevine communicates the experience, strength, and hope of its contributors and reflects a broad geographic spectrum of current AA experience with recovery, unity, and service. Founded in 1944, the Grapevine does not receive group contributions, but is supported entirely through magazine subscription sales and additional income derived from the sale of Grapevine items.

The awareness that every AA member has an individual way of working the program permeates the pages of the Grapevine, and throughout its history the magazine has been a forum for the varied and often divergent opinions of AAs around the world. Articles are not intended to be statements of AA policy, nor does publication of any article imply endorsement by either AA or the Grapevine.

As Bill W. expressed it in 1946, "The Grapevine will be the voice of the Alcoholics Anonymous movement. Its editors and staff will be primarily accountable to the AA movement as a whole. . . . Within the bounds of friendliness and good taste, the Grapevine will enjoy perfect freedom of speech on all matters directly pertaining to Alcoholics Anonymous. . . . Like the Alcoholics Anonymous movement it is to mirror, there will be but one central purpose: The Grapevine will try to carry the AA message to alcoholics and practice the AA principles in all its affairs."

Alcoholics Anonymous®

AA's program of recovery is fully set forth in its basic text, *Alcoholics Anonymous* (commonly known as the Big Book), now in its Fourth Edition, as well as in *Twelve Steps and Twelve Traditions* and other books. Information on AA can also be found on AA's website at www.aa.org, or by writing to: Alcoholics Anonymous, Box 459, Grand Central Station, New York, NY 10163. For local resources, check your local telephone directory under "Alcoholics Anonymous."

The AA Grapevine

The Grapevine is AA's international monthly journal, published continuously since its first issue in June 1944. The AA pamphlet on the Grapevine describes its scope and purpose this way: "As an integral part of Alcoholics Anonymous for almost sixty years, the Grapevine publishes articles that reflect the full diversity of experience and thought found within the AA Fellowship. No one viewpoint of philosophy dominates its pages, and in determining content, the editorial staff relies on the principles of the Twelve Traditions."

In addition to a monthly magazine, the Grapevine also produces anthologies, audiocassette tapes and audio CDs based on published articles, an annual wall calendar, and a pocket planner. The entire collection of Grapevine articles is available online in its Digital Archive. AA Grapevine also publishes La Viña, a Spanish-language recovery magazine.

For more information on the Grapevine, or to subscribe, please visit the magazine's website at www.aagrapevine.org, or write to:

The AA Grapevine
475 Riverside Drive, New York, NY 10115
For subscription information call:

English	1-800-631-6025 (US)
	1-800-734-5856 (International)
Spanish	1-800-640-8781 (US)
	1-800-734-5857 (International)

E-mail: gvcirculation@aagrapevine.org